My Amish

Indiana

Learning about
our Amish neighbors

by

Susan W. Mosey

1

To all my Amish friends
and acquaintances,
but especially to Glenn and Ruth

Table of Contents

Introduction

My husband Gary and I married in 2007, when we were in our fifties. It was my first marriage—I guess I'm a late bloomer!

By then I'd been visiting Elkhart and Lagrange Counties in northern Indiana since the mid-1980s with various friends and family, from my home in suburban Chicago, and I'd been fascinated with the Old Order Amish culture for longer than that. I'd had Amish friends in the area since the mid-1990s. I watched, listened, and asked a lot of questions.

In 2013 I started writing down my experiences and observations on my blog, and then on Facebook where I could share more photos.

So, we went to Amish Indiana on our honeymoon in 2007, and then Gary was hooked, too—and so "there" became "here" in 2017 when we sold our home in suburban Chicago and moved to Middlebury, Indiana. These days, both of us show visitors the area, doing both bus and private tours.

Since I first came here my network of Amish friends and acquaintances has grown, as I've watched kids become adults and adults start families of their own. I've shared in weddings, funerals, graduations, family nights, work frolics, buggy rides, and more. I learn something new nearly every day.

What I write here comes with a few caveats… Firstly: I write about what I personally know—thus the title of this book. And what I know is the Amish of Elkhart and Lagrange Counties in northern in Indiana—the third largest Amish settlement in the country. Details differ in other Amish settlements—and there are hundreds of them in the United States and Canada.

Secondly: What I write is what I've seen and heard firsthand. I don't claim to be an expert on all things Amish, nor do I even claim to describe all 28,000 folks in this settlement. I'll try to answer the questions I had when I first came here, and the questions Gary and I get asked when we give tours of the area.

Thirdly: Be wary of what you see on TV or read on the internet about the Amish. Enough said about that.

My Amish friends know about my writing, and it has their blessing. I print out my stories, and they like to pass them around. As one said to me, "Finally… someone is telling the truth about us."

Well, I'll do my best.

BEGINNINGS
AND
BACKSTORIES

How It Started

I feel like I've been visiting Amish Indiana forever, but actually it started in 1985. I was a teacher in suburban Chicago, and our staff went to South Bend, Indiana, every fall for a teachers' convention. At a rest area along the tollway one particular year, my friend Becky picked up a brochure for a country inn near Amish country. She said, "We should do this next year after the convention! We could spend the weekend and go shopping."

So the next fall, we did just that—and every fall thereafter for a decade. And that began my love affair with Lagrange and Elkhart Counties—Amish Indiana. I came back to visit again and again over the years—at first once a year, then twice a year... I am not fond of driving on the tollways, but I always had one friend or another who was willing to drive.

Sometimes we would stay at the big Amish-style inns, but usually we would find little B&B (Bed and Breakfast) places. It was nice to have a local to ask for advice on where to eat, where to shop, where to find things.

At first I spent most of my time in the shops—but as the years went on, I had more stuff than I needed. Then I started going just to soak up the atmosphere. Sometimes I sat at the Friday morning horse auction for hours to watch them sell the big Belgian work horses and the smaller, sleeker buggy horses. Sometimes I sat in a rocking chair at Yoder's Department Store and, hidden behind my sunglasses, I watched the people go by. Sometimes I went to the auction barn, which fascinated me. Sometimes I brought home a piece of furniture or other decor. Sometimes a long drive through the countryside was just what I needed.

And always, there was the food. Good old-fashioned food, like my grandmother used to make. Locally grown beef and chicken… Locally made bread and pies… Food items that I could find only in Amish country. I brought it home by the bagful.

Then in 2007, a big change—I got married. What would my new husband think of my favorite place? Would he think it was boring, or would he understand what I saw in it? It didn't take long for him to make up his mind… I think what first won him over was the food, and all the rest was just icing on the cake. Now it seems like we've always gone there together.

My husband and I hope to retire there in a few years—how wonderful that he shares my love of Amish Indiana! When he first suggested retiring there, I thought, "What? Leave my life in Illinois and start over?" But now I am looking forward to it more than I can say. It suits me. It suits us.

Postscript:
I wrote the above post in April 2013. In late 2016, Gary and I bought a home in Middlebury, Indiana—near the heart of Amish Country—and we moved there in 2017.

Across Cultural Lines:
My Friendship with the Amish

By the late 1990s I had been visiting Amish Indiana with various friends and relatives for fifteen years. There were a handful of B&Bs that had become favorites, and I tried to visit at least twice a year, soaking up the local atmosphere and shopping for things for my home.

One summer I brought my nine-year old niece Amy for a visit, along with a friend and her daughter. Our B&B owner had become friends with her Amish neighbors over the years, and since we were staying over a Sunday (rare for visitors, since nothing is open on Sunday)— she said, "My Amish neighbor sometimes takes my" English" guests for buggy rides after church. Do you think your niece would like that?"

So the next afternoon, Gerald (as I now know him) pulled up in his buggy, and we took a ride. It was wonderful! A buggy goes just the right speed to see the countryside—fast enough for a constant change in scenery, but slow enough not to miss anything. I was totally smitten.

The next morning the four of us bought a Yoder's Department Store gift certificate and a thank you card. We wrote some notes on the card and drove over to deliver it to their farm. I wasn't sure what I'd do with it if no one came to the door—but Rebecca (as I now know her) came out and, after we explained our errand, said the last thing I expected: "Would you like to come in and have some lemonade?"

I had read everything I could find on the Amish during those early years, and I didn't see this one coming. They do business with "the English" (as they call us), but socializing with us—that isn't so common.

Before long, Amy had disappeared with Rebecca's children, not to be seen for the rest of the morning. She fed livestock, hauled firewood on a wagon, and just generally had more fun than a girl from suburban Los Angeles could imagine. She even met a cow named Amy! When she came back with cow manure on her shoes, and Rebecca had to hose it off, Amy said, "Cow manure! I can't wait to tell the kids at school!"

That was about twenty-five years ago... Rebecca's eight children, who all lived at home then, are all married now. I've been to five of their family's weddings, and six of their family came to mine. I know their extended family and some of their friends, and they have met more of my and friends as well. My niece Amy even came back recently—as woman in her thirties now—and spent an evening there. Rebecca and Gerald and I have shared laughter and sorrow—and always, lots of good food!

I still don't know what they saw in me, or why they allowed me into their world. But I have learned that friendship is friendship, across cultural lines—and this friendship is a "keeper."

The Backstory of a Unique Culture

I've done a bus tour and a couple of private tours already this year as I write this, and I've been surprised at how many people want a little backstory on where exactly the Amish came from. For that, we go back to Switzerland in the 1500s...

In 1525, shortly after the Protestant Reformation began, a group of Christians emerged in Switzerland who refused to have their babies baptized, believing in adult choice in religion, and therefore, adult baptism instead. Since baptism was the equivalent of receiving church membership, Swiss citizenship, membership on the tax rolls (like our Social Security numbers), and registration for the draft—this was seen as radical and disruptive.

This group came to be known as "Anabaptists" and they were severely persecuted. Hundreds were executed—burned, drowned, tortured publicly, and starved in dungeons. Even today, most Amish households have a copy of the book "The Martyr's Mirror," which records many of these stories.

Needless to say, the Amish soon retreated to more remote areas of Switzerland, and eventually to the Alsace region of what is now southern France. Their desire for "separation from the world" and nonconformity to mainstream culture became more and more ingrained.

It was in 1693 in Alsace that the Anabaptists split into two groups: The Amish, led by Jacob Amman, and the Swiss Brethren (later known as Mennonites), led by Menno Simons. There were various doctrinal disagreements that drove them apart, one of the main ones being shunning—which the Mennonites felt was too harsh, but the Amish felt was necessary for the purity and unity of their church.

In the early 1700s William Penn was granted a piece of land in North America which came to be known as Pennsylvania, as a place for the persecuted Quakers of England to make a fresh start. Penn invited the good Amish farmers of Alsace to join him, and eventually some of the Pennsylvania Amish moved west to Ohio and then Indiana. The Amish church eventually died out in Europe.

Today the Amish are found in 32 states and Canada. There are about 375,000 of them, and they are thriving! 80 to 90 per cent of their children remain in the faith, and their population is doubling approximately every 20 years. There are many subdivisions now from the main body of Old Order Amish, including the Beachy Amish, the yellow buggy (Byler) Amish, the white buggy (Nebraska) Amish, the Swartzentruber Amish, and the New Order Amish.

For more on the history of the Amish, try Donald Kraybill's small but info-packed book "Simply Amish." Don't be fooled by its small size; I had to read it twice to even begin to absorb it all!

For a deeper dive, try Steven Nolt's "A History of the Amish." Here's a quote I think is very illuminating: "While Moderns are preoccupied with 'finding themselves,' the Amish are engaged in 'losing themselves... It's about submission—to God, to others, and to the church." No wonder they don't always think or act like we do!

For more on the Indiana Amish, try Meyers and Nolt's "An Amish Patchwork," written in 2004. There are a number of other Amish settlements in Indiana, and not all are just like the one where I live. The Amish and other old order groups in the rest of Indiana are actually quite diverse.

The Story of Two Towns and a Feud

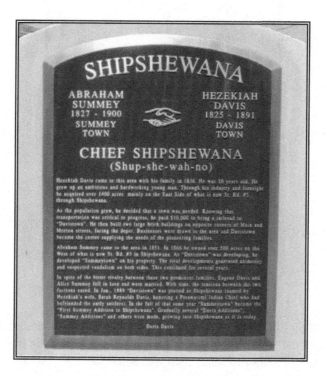

This plaque sits at an intersection in downtown Shipshewana, at the corner of Main and Morton Streets. It tells the story of how Shipshewana was founded as the result of a Hatfields-and-McCoys-type feud, and the love story that ended it.

We start with two pioneers: Hezekiah Davis and Abraham Summey. Both dreamed of building a town along what is now State Road 5, which runs north and south through present-day Shipshewana. And both had the money and the land to make it happen.

Hezekiah Davis owned 1,400 acres of land on the east side of what is now State Road 5, from north to south for a mile and a half.

His rival, Abraham Summey, owned 500 acres of land across State Road 5 on the west side, from north to south for a mile. I found a picture of Mr. Davis, but none of Mr. Summey, if that gives you an idea of who the eventual victor is going to be...

Hezekiah Davis

NEWBURY TP.

So Abraham Summey began laying out a town on a 40-acre piece of land along the west side of the road— picture it where the gas station now stands. Neither of these men was self-effacing—Abraham called his creation "Summey Town."

Hezekiah Davis began building "Davis Town" across the road to the east, where most of the downtown shops are now found on Harrison Street.

But Davis didn't want his town anywhere near Summey's. So he left a 150-foot-wide strip of vacant land on his side of State Road 5, and he allowed nothing to be built there—thus creating a north-south "no man's land" between the two towns! Picture it where the Blue Gate Restaurant now stands, running north to the grain elevators.

According to the historical information on the town of Shipshewana website, the rival developments "generated animosity and suspected vandalism on both sides." I'd like to know more about that!

What could heal this rift? Nothing short of a Romeo-and-Juliet love story (but with a much happier ending). Hezekiah's son, Eugene Davis, fell in love with Abraham's daughter, Alice Summey, and in

1877 they were married. According to later census records, they had ten children, nine of whom survived childhood.

After that, the tensions between the two sides eased considerably. But there were still two rival towns…. But Davis had an ace up his sleeve. He realized how important transportation was to the development of his town, so in 1888 he paid the whopping sum of $10,000 to bring the railroad through, on the Davis Town side.

Davis Town was officially incorporated that year. At the suggestion of Hezekiah's wife Sarah, the new town was named "Shipshewana" after the late local Pottawatomie Indian chief. (The Pottawatomies had been driven away years earlier to reservations in Kansas, but that's another story, which can also be found on the Town of Shipshewana website.)

Davis having the railroad on his side of the great divide meant the kiss of death for Summey Town… Just a year later, the Summey Town land was annexed into the new town of Shipshewana.

After the death of Hezekiah Davis three years later in 1891, the wide strip of land between the two towns was laid out in lots and sold at auction—the official end of the feud at last, I suppose.

Miller, Yoder, Bontrager:
The Pennsylvania Dutch and the Swiss Amish

Miller, Yoder, Bontrager… Names you see on mailboxes and businesses all over Amish Indiana. Lately I did a little research into the most common names here. That led me into learning about the two distinct Amish ethnic groups found in Indiana today. (I am indebted to the book "An Amish Patchwork" by Thomas Meyers and Steven Nolt for helping me to get the details right.)

The main Amish group in Indiana, the one found in Lagrange and Elkhart Counties, is the "Pennsylvania Dutch." They are descendants of Germans who settled in Pennsylvania in the 1700s. They were called "Pennsylvania German" or "Pennsylvania Dutch," and they spoke a form of German called by the same name. The Amish among them retained the old language, but the non-Amish lost it.

Then in the 1800s, the western Pennsylvania Amish began migrating to Holmes County, Ohio, and then into northern Indiana, and today they make up the third largest Amish settlement in America. The most common surnames in this settlement are Miller, Yoder,

Bontrager, Hostetler, Lehman, and Lambright. Their language is still called "Pennsylvania Dutch" or just simply "Dutch." (It is quite different from both present-day German and Dutch.) These are the Amish I am familiar with.

But there was a second stream of Amish into Indiana in the mid-1800s. They came directly from Switzerland and settled further south in Indiana, around Fort Wayne. Their most common surnames are different—Schwartz, Hilty, Graber, Lengacher, Schmucker, and Eicher. They are the Swiss Amish, and their Amish dialect is commonly called "Swiss."

The two groups don't have very much interaction, and tend not to intermarry or live in the same communities. An Amish friend once told me that the two dialects are so different that they have to switch to English to be able to communicate!

The Swiss Amish tend to be more conservative than the their Amish brethren further north. For example, have always driven only open buggies, even in the winter (although that is starting to change). They are more conservative in matters of dress, housing, and lifestyle. They mark their graves with simple wooden stakes instead of stone markers. And, remarkably, they still practice yodeling!

Getting back to the northern Indiana Amish: A funny thing about the "Pennsylvania Dutch" language is that it is a spoken language only. Their written language is English.

Thus, my Amish friends are actually tri-lingual... They learn "Dutch" as their first language, and it is the language they speak at home and socially. They learn English (spoken and written) when they enter school at age seven. And they learn the old "High German" in school, since it is the language of their Bible and hymnbook (the Ausbund). Luckily for me, they switch back and forth easily!

SUNDAYS

Getting Ready for a Lot of Company

A few Sundays ago, it was time for my friends Emmon and Lily to take their turn hosting church—an event that happens once or twice a year for most Amish families.

Church can be held in a barn, a shop building, a large open basement, or even a tent in the yard. All they need is an area big enough to set up the benches in the traditional way.

Lots and lots of cleaning takes place in the week leading up to church Sunday! Emmon had been busy cleaning out the shop building, power washing the cement, and lots of other tasks. Lily and her sisters and other women of the family had been cleaning the house top to bottom, raking the yard, and otherwise making everything shine. Hosting church is a very big deal in Amish Indiana, and everyone wants to make sure they put their best foot forward.

I happened to stop by the day before, and Emmon and Lily let me take a few photos. As you can see in the picture, the shop building, where they normally keep their buggies and other miscellany, had been cleared out and cleaned up. In the back on the left is the area for the married men and young boys (under sixteen) to sit, with the two preachers, deacon, and bishop in the front row. Often there are visiting preachers from other church districts—church is held every other week, allowing for lots of visiting—so the front two rows may be taken up with them.

In the back of the photo on the right sit the married women and small children and the younger girls (under sixteen). Notice the half-row of comfy chairs in the front, for the older ladies!

The young unmarried men sit in the rows at bottom left, and the young unmarried women in the rows at the bottom right.

The bench wagon sat nearby, along with buggies which had to be moved outside to clear the shop building for church. (More about bench wagons later.)

I drove by on Sunday morning and took the picture below of buggies in the temporary parking lot next to the shop building—an area that had been mowed the day before just for this purpose.

After the three-hour church service, everyone gathers for a meal. The meal has a set menu, in order to avoid the hostesses feeling pressured to compete to outdo each other:

- Bread (often homemade)
- Ham
- Cheese
- Maybe egg salad
- Regular butter

- Amish church peanut butter (more on that in the food chapter)
- Jelly or jam
- Canned pickles and beets
- Coffee (the Amish drink it black) and water
- Cookies for dessert

Sometimes the adults sit around under a shady tree and talk all afternoon, while the children play and the young people socialize. The Sabbath is taken seriously here, and no unnecessary work is ever done on Sunday. It's a day of rest and socializing and worship.

Enough Seating for the Whole Neighborhood

So… the Amish don't have church buildings, but rather, they take turns hosting church, which is held once every two weeks. A family typically will host church twice a year. One of the things that makes this easier is the bench wagon.

Recently I was hanging out with some Amish friends in Goshen, Indiana, and they had a brand-new bench wagon sitting in their yard. They offered to show me how it was arranged, and they said it was fine if I took photos. They didn't have to tell me twice! I'd been intrigued by bench wagons for years.

Here's how it works: Each church district has their own horse-drawn bench wagon. The wagon is taken to wherever church (or some other event, like a wedding or funeral or school program) is going to be held. Everything is organized for easy storage.

The heart of the bench wagon is the benches! They are stored in the back. The number on the end of the bench tells how many feet long it is. There are two fold-down uprights, one on each end of the bench, so setup is easy. On this new bench wagon, the shelves are carpeted, and there is a chart on the left back door which shows how to store them properly and how many there should be.

The side and front doors of the wagon hold more goodies—everything needed to host and conduct a church service.

The Ausbund, or hymnal, is the same one that the Amish have used for hundreds of years. It is written in old German, much like Shakespearean English—very different from the "Dutch" that the Amish speak as their first and main language. The hymnals are stored in tough plastic boxes with handy lifting slots cut into them.

This bench wagon belongs to church district #71-2, so everything in the wagon carries that number. Everything looked very fresh and new—because this was a recently-formed church district, so the wagon and everything in it was recently purchased and assembled.

After a three-hour church service, there is always a meal. The bench wagon contains all the plastic dishes, flatware, coffee pots, etc. needed to serve a congregation of 25-35 families plus guests, all organized and labeled.

The bench wagon is an idea that works well, and I was glad to see one up close!

Buying a Mutza Suit

I was in a general store in Shipshewana a few months ago, waiting for someone to finish some shopping. I started taking a look at the "Sunday suits" that Amishmen wear for church, weddings, and funerals.

All of them are made in the same style, and always in black with a white shirt. Some women make them for their husbands and sons, but they are more complicated than the typical Amish clothes, so often they are purchased off-the-rack or custom made. They are very well made, I noticed, with quality materials and linings and a high quality of construction, so they are not inexpensive!

The suit is called a "mutza" in the Pennsylvania Dutch language. The long-sleeved white oxford shirt is much like an English dress shirt, and is typically store-bought.

The jacket differs from an typical English men's suit in the plain collar and the lack of front buttons or outside pockets. (Hooks and eyes are used to fasten the jacket.) The Amish avoid buttons on nearly all clothing except the small buttons on children's clothing and boys/men's shirts, as buttons represented the military back in Switzerland and Germany, and the Amish were often persecuted for their refusal to serve in the military.

The pants differ the most from an English men's suit. Like all Amishmen's pants, they are an old style called "broadfall pants"—which is to say, they are not closed by a fly, but rather by four buttons across the top of a large panel. Suspenders are worn with the pants, not a belt.

The vest is an important part of the ensemble. In hot weather, the jacket is taken off or not worn—just the vest, which is much cooler. I noticed that the price tag on the vest was $79.95.

Black dress shoes and socks complete the outfit, along with a black felt hat. I have noticed that the hats run about $120 and are very high quality. The men take very good care of them! These felt hats are worn only for dress occasions.

Driving by a church gathering, wedding, or funeral and seeing the dozens of men and boys in their black and white dress clothes is very impressive. Much expense and care go into their Sunday clothes, and it shows.

A Sunday Night Singing

For years Gary and I have driven our young Amish friends to their Sunday night singings occasionally. Last Sunday I finally got my first chance to attend one.

This is a weekly tradition for many Amish young people. These gatherings are held all over the Michiana area (northeastern Indiana and southern Michigan) in about a dozen locations on any given Sunday night. They usually involve half an hour of eating (typically 6:00-6:30) and then an hour of singing. After that, the kids go their separate ways fairly quickly, since Monday is a work day, and work starts early around here.

I got my chance because it was my friend Rebecca's daughter's turn to host the singing for their area, and Grandma was helping with the food.

The location was a few miles north of the Michigan state line in-the Centreville Amish settlement—about 12 to 14 church districts who used to have two youth groups for Sunday night singings, but recently merged into one. Around 100 young people were expected, and that's about how many showed up.

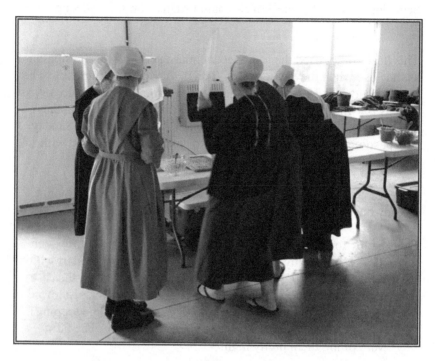

When I say "young people," or as the Amish say, "youngies," this would be youth who are sixteen years old, up through marriage age. A few of the youngies have passed their 30th birthday, but since they're still single and still hoping to meet their soulmate, here they are! There's not really an age limit.

Most "youngies" have a particular youth group/singing that they attend regularly, although they're free to visit other ones as they wish. The various youth groups/gatherings have their own names—including the Bluebirds, Heartland, Twilight, the Seagulls, the Wildflowers, the Bons, Lakeside, and Clearspring. The Bluebirds had gotten too big for one space in recent years, so that group recently split, with the younger members (roughly those under 25) forming the Heartland group.

You can always tell where a singing is being held on a Sunday evening… Buggies, bicycles, pedestrians, and hired vans converge from every direction on the chosen location. Some singings have as many as 200 kids or more in attendance! Some groups are known for being more conservative than others. Kids who are into the wilder behavior typical of some Amish youth usually don't attend singings at all.

This host family used the same recent house addition for the singing as they use when they host church (which they did last Sunday). The family hosting the singing uses the benches from the bench wagon, as well as flatware and other supplies. The host dad told me that the setup is about the same as he used when hosting church last Sunday, except some of the longer benches on one side were replaced with shorter ones to make room for the food tables.

Rebecca and I got there at 5:00, and there were half a dozen moms already busy in the kitchen preparing for the 6:00 meal.

I was happy to see that the main dish for the evening was "Mexican haystacks" – one of my favorite Amish meals! Haystacks start with a base layer, then moving layer after layer is piled on top. In the case of Mexican haystacks, the base layer is crumbled crackers, followed by taco-seasoned ground beef, then the typical taco veggie toppings, then crumbled tortilla chips, with nacho cheese on top. The farm boys were piling them pretty high!

At 6:30 sharp, the singing began. The guys sat on one side of the room and the girls on the other side, both sides facing the divider in the middle. Some singings still do it the older way, with the kids sitting at long tables, boys on one side of the tables and girls on the other side. But this youth group, like so many this area, has grown too large for that type of setup.

Each young person typically has two hymnbooks (*Heartland* and *Mountain Laurel*), most of the songs in English but a few in the back in Old German, and they take turns choosing a song. Some are sung in two part harmony, some in four. Many of the songs involve an echo effect where the guys and girls weave in and out of the song in turn.

There was a table of dads off to the side, discussing whatever Amishmen discuss when they get together. The moms and I sat in the back. A few younger kids were playing in the yard.

Some Amish sheet music makes use of our regular rounded musical notes, but some use an older form of music called "shape notes." An example of shape note music is shown here.

After an hour of singing, things wrapped up pretty quickly. The half dozen moms went over to the food tables, packed up the leftovers, set up dishpans, and washed all the silverware on the spot. I was impressed by how many of the young people took the time to walk up to the mother who hosted the event to say thanks.

GETTING HITCHED

An Amish Love Story

I was out singing for the elderly Mrs. R. a few weeks ago (more on her later) and I heard the most wonderful love story!

I worked on her family's genealogy a while back, and I noticed that her late husband was from Lancaster County, Pennsylvania. It's rare for someone from Lancaster County to end up here in Amish Indiana—so I was curious and asked the family how that came to be. Mrs. R. has a hard time talking due to her stroke, but her daughter-in-law filled me in while Mrs. R. listened and smiled. Out of that conversation came the most amazing story...

The year was 1958. Three young Amishmen from Lancaster County were traveling west on a vacation to California to see the redwoods— Hank, Frank, and Eli. Eli's mother had made him promise to stop in Indiana on their way out west, to visit an uncle who lived in Nappanee.

While in Shipshewana, Eli decided to go to the Sunday night singing being held nearby for the local young people. (These singings are one of the main social mixers for young unmarried Amish.) While there, he met a young lady who instantly captured his heart.

Eli knew at once that he had found what he was looking for. So did she, apparently, because when Eli asked her if he could see her home that evening, she let her boyfriend Sam know that she wouldn't be needing his help getting home that night. In spite of her stroke, she managed to tell me that she still remembers the look on Sam's face!

Eli told his young traveling companions to go on out west without him—but they ended up heading back to Pennsylvania instead. Eli returned with them, but not before starting up a friendship with the young lady that was carried on with letters and visits back and forth for the next two years.

As things got serious, she wondered what it would be like to leave family and friends and start life with Eli in Pennsylvania—an area where the Amish dress a bit differently and live by slightly different rules. She was ready to do so—but it turned out not to be a decision she had to make. Eli was perfectly willing to settle down in northern Indiana. He soon moved out to Indiana and lived with an Amish bishop named Yoder and his family.

The young couple got married in 1960, and before long they bought a farm near Shipshewana, where Eli made his living as a carpenter. They had thirteen children together (twelve surviving) and lived happily for nearly thirty years, until his death from a heart attack in 1990.

The Day Before the Wedding

A few months ago one of my Amish friends was one of a group of women who were cooks for a wedding. It takes a large team of cooks (about 40) to get this done, since a typical all-day Amish wedding event involves serving around 1,000 meals over the course of the day! These days, the team of cooks all wear matching dresses on the big day, in a fabric chosen by the bride.

The other cooks had arrived by buggy, but my friend lived too far away, so after I drove her there, I got a chance to look around. One farm building and a large rented tent were used as the food preparation areas. I wanted to stay out of their way (and I couldn't have taken pictures of them anyway), so I headed over to the building being used for the post-wedding dinner. Here the tables were already laid out.

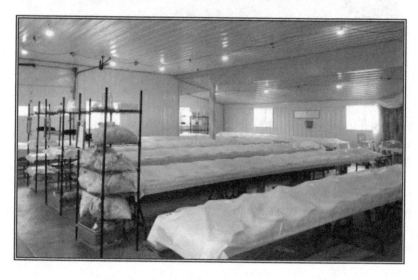

Nearby were racks holding additional rented china—after the first seating, there would be three more during the course of the day. Nearly everything needed for such a large event can be rented.

An Amish bride and groom choose ten or twelve pairs of young men and women to be "table waiters" for their wedding. This means a long day of work, but it is an honor to be chosen. Each pair of table waiters has specific assigned tables to take care of—usually one long connected row of them. I saw menus posted all over the room, at the different serving stations, helping the waiters know what to do and when. The menu can vary slightly for the different sittings. The waiters responsible for each station might also change for the various meal sittings.

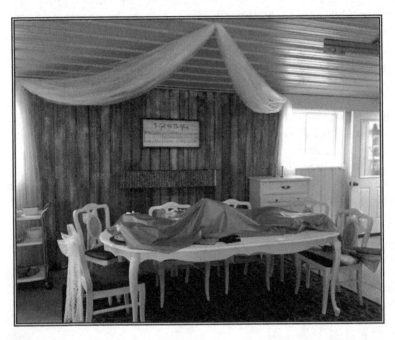

I stopped to look at the elevated table where the wedding party would sit—bride, groom, and two pairs of witnesses. It had been done up beautifully in silver and white.

How is so much food cooked in a farmhouse kitchen? It isn't. A wedding wagon (or two) is rented, which contains multiple stoves, refrigerators, and sinks. The day of the wedding, the hot food can be prepared there.

The entire farm was a beehive of activity, as the men did their part to prepare for parking many dozens of buggies, bicycles, and probably a few cars, and other outdoor tasks, and the women prepared the food. The bride circulated around, taking time to introduce herself to me before heading out to the lane to talk to her groom.

I was amazed at the organization, the teamwork, and most of all, the overall atmosphere of calm!

A Spring Wedding, Part One:
The Church Service and Noon Meal

I recently went to another Amish wedding—I think it was my sixth.

I arrived early and followed the signs for "car parking". Nearby, in the field between the farm where the wedding would take place and the bride's home (where the meals would take place) there was a pasture filling up quickly with buggies on one side, and horses on the other side.

There were rented tents everywhere. Tents are needed for staging areas, cooking, and sometimes for the opening of the gifts. Bench wagons from several church districts are there, along with rented "wedding wagons" containing extra stoves, ovens, freezers, and refrigerators. Dishes and flatware are also rented and have arrived a few days earlier in sturdy wooden boxes. It was a beehive of activity.

A bit before 9 a.m., the invited guests began filing in. There's a form as to how this is done—men and women separately, and oldest to youngest, to put it simply. I sometimes end up being seated with the English guests, but this time I was seated with the Amish aunties and grandmas in the second row, which I really liked. As people filed in, they passed by and greeted the couple and their "witnesses" who were seated on a bench in the back. When the service began, those six moved to seats in the very front.

The guests were seated in the usual "U" shape, with the men on one side, the women on the other side, the young people at the bottom of the U, and the speaker at the top of the U. There were empty rows of benches reserved for the cooks and table waiters to come in for the last hour so they wouldn't miss the actual wedding ceremony. I didn't take any pictures, since photography of people is not allowed in the Amish tradition.

The wedding is like a typical Amish church service—three hours long, all in Pennsylvania Dutch. At the end, the bride and groom step forward with their witnesses for the ceremony, which lasts about ten minutes. Wedding rings are not exchanged; the Amish don't wear jewelry, not even wedding rings or wrist watches.

After the ceremony, we all filed out into the open air to walk across the field to the bride's home farm, where the meals would be served.

Usually there are four seatings over the course of the day. The noon seating is for those who attended the service. The second seating, around 3 p.m., is for those who helped prepare and serve the food, as well as family members and other helpers who haven't had a spare moment all day to sit down and eat! The third seating is at 5:00 or 5:30 p.m., and it's for a few hundred more friends and relatives who couldn't attend the wedding service. The fourth seating is at 7:00 p.m., for the young adults. Over a thousand meals are typically served!

The bridal party sat at a special table at one end with their families nearby. The rest of the guests sat at 12 very long tables, men at one end and women at the other. Luckily for my husband and I, an Amish couple we knew "adopted" each of us! Sometimes there is a separate table for English guests, but there were so few at this wedding that we were mixed in. The Amish guests near us spoke mostly English as a courtesy to us. Each table had its own pair of table waiters (one male, one female), wearing matching shirts and dresses.

Being here reminded me of another wedding which I attended last summer… The Amish drink their coffee black. I forgot about that fact, and asked one of the servers for some sugar and cream. He looked baffled—which caused me to say, "Never mind!" But a few minutes later, the mother of the bride came around with sugar and cream, which she had gone to the house to fetch, just for me. Well, that was embarrassing!

Anyway—after the noon meal, there was another flurry of activity as the guests congratulated the couple and filed outside. Immediately, the table waiters and other helpers took up the dirty dishes, cleaned them on the spot (table by table), and reset the tables. There would be three more meals served that day!

Normally the a.m. guests stay as long as they like after lunch, the adults socializing, the young people playing volleyball, and the younger kids running around having fun. But I had work to do, which I'll talk about in the next chapter.

A Spring Wedding, Part Two:
Barbeque Sauce and Bacon

This is the second chapter about a wedding I attended recently. The day wasn't over for me after the wedding and noon meal! My invitation had indicated that, for the first time ever, I was also invited to the third official seating—at 7:00 p.m. This is the young people's seating, and it involves singing after the meal. (The groom had rightly guessed that I would enjoy it.)

But lots of things happened before that…

I had told the family that I'd be available to take care of any emergencies, and the first one happened before the wedding even began. The mother of the bride came and found me with a problem—the chicken barbeque team, who had been working all night, was out of Sweet Baby Ray's! They had gone through four gallons already, and needed two more.

I was dispatched to go down to E&S Foods in Shipshewana and pick up some more sauce… An hour later, mission accomplished!

I made it back in time for the start of the ceremony… but half an hour in, a family member crept in and motioned me to follow her out. Turns out one of the groom's sisters needed to rush home for something she'd forgotten. (Actually, her toddler had made off with it and she found it on the living room floor.) So I drove her home and back and then rejoined the church service.

After the service everyone walked across an open field from a neighbor's home to the bride's home for the noon meal. But as soon as I got back, someone asked if I could take my car back over and bring back an older woman who couldn't walk very well, which I did.

So then came the noon meal, which I talked about in the last chapter…

Afterward, I decided to go home until the 7 p.m. seating. I'd talked to all the people I knew, and I wanted to go home and play with my puppy. But before I left, I asked if anything else was needed, and the groom sent me out to get twelve pounds of bacon. So back to E&S I went. I talked to a manager and got it added to the bride's father's account.

The evening singing was wonderful. I thought I'd be stashed in an inconspicuous corner, which would have been fine, but I was seated with the young people, across from a young man I know quite well. There were eight tables of 25 apiece, so about 200 young people attended.

They have a special old custom for the evening seating; some wedding parties follow it, and some don't. First the couples married six months or less file into the dining area. Then the dating couples file in. Lastly, the single and unattached young people fall in line as random boy-and-girl couples and file in. That last part wasn't done here—the young men entered the dining area single file, as did the young women. Everyone sits at the tables in this same order, with girls on one side of the long tables and boys on the other side.

The table servers from the previous seatings, being mostly young people, were now free to sit down and join the meal and singing. Married couples related to the family did most of the table serving.

After the meal (which had a slightly different menu than the noon meal), the singing began. The songs were found in a special booklet we were given. The booklet also listed the wedding party and had a special message for the guests. Most of the songs were in English, and I was able to sing along. For the one with the verses in Old German (the language of their Bible and hymnal), I just listened and tried to follow along!

After half an hour of singing, the evening ended. Before leaving, the young people stood up one table at a time and filed by the wedding party's table, offering congratulations and leaving gifts. (Most of the young people give cash gifts.)

Almost immediately, an army of volunteers materialized and began dis-assembling the entire wedding reception venue. Tables were cleared in a matter of minutes and the food team began washing and drying the dishes, table by table, with military precision.

Then benches and tables began to disappear, followed by nearly everything else in the room and surrounding tents. Benches were loaded into the bench wagons, dishes were carefully repacked into their wooden crates, and within an hour, thanks to the multitude of help, you'd never know a full day of celebration had just taken place there!

I do hope, dear reader, that you enjoyed hearing more about Amish weddings. In the Amish culture, marriage is for life, and I hope that this couple will have a lifetime of happy memories of this special day.

SPECIAL PEOPLE

Wheelchair Mary

Polio.

We think of it as ancient history—a disease that was long ago eradicated. But that's not true—It was widespread around 1950, so there are quite a few Americans still living with it, including around ten to fifteen in the Amish community where I live.

Earlier this year I did something I've been wanting to do for a long time… I spent some time with Wheelchair Mary (as she calls herself). Mary is the only surviving wheelchair-bound polio victim in this area, and I wanted to hear her story.

Mary told me it started one morning when she was 18 months old—in 1952. Her mother came in to get her out of bed, and Mary (who was a vigorous walker by then) couldn't stand up in her crib. Her mother knew immediately what was wrong… Eight other young children in their church district already had polio. One of them, a little boy, died while visiting relatives in Iowa and was brought home in a casket.

As Mary told me, "America was rich with polio in the early 50s, before the vaccine." She says adults who got it typically died, but children usually didn't. The doctors didn't even know what to recommend… Keep them warm? Cool them off? Try to make them exercise their limbs? Make them rest?

Eventually, with funds from the March of Dimes, Mary was sent to the polio hospital in Warm Springs, Georgia when she was five years old. (This hospital was founded by President Franklin Delano Roosevelt in 1927, and he continued to go there until his death in 1945.)

Mary lived in a ward which held 25 young girls—5 rows of 5 beds each. She spent seven months at the hospital, separated from her family and everything she had ever known. Her mother had packed her Amish clothes, but the hospital clothed her like the other girls, since she was the only Amish patient and they didn't want her to feel awkward.
Since only English was spoken there, Mary quickly picked it up, and before long she entirely lost her ability to speak Pennsylvania Dutch, so she had to relearn it from scratch when she returned home. She

44

said that when her father came to get her, she was shocked to see that, unlike the men at the hospital, he had a long beard! Upon returning home, her closest sister, Irene, didn't believe this English-speaking girl was her dear sister and said to their parents, "Let's go find the real Mary!"

While she was at Warm Springs Mary was encouraged to use her braces and crutches in order to keep her spine strong. She had a variety of therapies while she was there. Her knee and hip muscles had contracted to the point that she was losing her ability to stand up, so she also had surgery there to release them. Quite a lot for a five-year-old girl to endure, far away from home!

Her brother Mervin got polio in 1955—three years after Mary did. It didn't affect his legs or arms, but it nearly destroyed his mind. He spent the rest of his life under the care of his family, living with Mary in his later years, and he died a few years ago. No one else in the family was affected.

Mary said her school days were a struggle, as you can imagine. She "walked" with braces and crutches in those days, but she says her arms did all the work and her legs were useless. She went to Honeyville Elementary School for the first four years. But grades 5 to 9 were on the second floor—so she and her closest sister, Irene, were transferred to Topeka Elementary School. (There were no Amish schools yet.) She says the other seven girls in her class would take turns helping her—but many times they would forget and leave her outside at the end of recess!

Besides using her braces and crutches, the other kids pulled her around in a little red wagon that was obtained just for that purpose. Then in sixth grade she got a "school wheelchair" (she already had one at home), and she says that helped a lot. But Mary wanted to run, jump, and play with the other kids. She said she often sat off to the side with a lump in her throat, crying on the inside.

As a youth, she couldn't go to the Sunday night singings and other social events, and she says that made her rebellious inside. She said she was fifty years old before it stopped bothering her. I remarked, "It's hard to be different"—and Mary said, "Yes, you hit the nail on the head!" She says it's been a lifelong struggle to let go.

What is Mary's life like today? After the death of her father, she and her mother and her disabled brother moved into a lovely new home on the property of relatives, where Mary continued to live alone after the passing of her mother and brother. A few months ago she moved into a smaller place, an annex to the main house on the same farm, custom-built for her by family members who live in the main house. Her niece's dog Cody spends some of his time there, keeping Mary company. Mary's food is supplied by friends and neighbors who bring her frozen leftovers to heat up, which works out well for her.

A garage area near Mary's home contains her special wheelchair buggy and also her "road scooter" on which she can travel a couple of miles, to go to church or to visit people. (Quite a few of her family members live within that distance.) She told me she can get out of bed and into a wheelchair on her own, but she said, "It takes about twenty steps to do it!"

Mary's life has definitely had meaning... I was stunned to see a copy of the large book that she has authored. With the help of an expert Old-German-to-English translator, she has created an amazing resource for the Amish community—a large reference book on the rituals, songs, prayers, articles of faith, and other treasured documents of the Amish church, translated from the Old German into modern English, side-by-side on the pages.

This incredible project took Mary twenty years to complete. The first edition was published in 2000, with a revised edition in 2008. The large 568-page book includes translations of things such as these:

- The Amish Articles of Faith
- Passages of Scripture
- Translations of hymns from the Ausbund (Amish hymnal)
- Prayers of every kind and for every occasion
- Plenty of German-to-English word lists
- Wedding, funeral, and communion services
- The vows for marriage and church membership.

One time as a child, Mary sat watching a ball game with her father—she loved watching and cheering, but longed to play. Her father told her, "Don't look so sad—try to always wear a cheerful smile. Then people will come to you—since you can't go to them." She said it was good advice… and as she told me, "Many times, you just have to be a good listener!" When asked if her days seem long, she said, "No! No, not at all!" Mary said she still has lots of visitors—which today included my friend Rebecca and me. It was one of the best ways I've spent a morning in a very long time.

Ralph Bontrager and the Cheese House

Near our new home town of Middlebury, Indiana, is County Road 16, which becomes 250N when we cross the county line between Elkhart and Lagrange Counties... It's a road my husband calls the Cheese House Road.

This building is "The Cheese House"—which has had three names over the years—Deutsch Kase Haus, Guggisberg Cheese, and now, Heritage Ridge Creamery. It's more than a prize-winning cheese factory and retail shop, though—it has a backstory.

The year was 1977, and Indiana had just changed its regulations for dairy farming. In those days, hundreds of local dairy farmers (most of them Amish) produced milk the old fashioned way. Cows were still milked by hand, and the milk was stored in 10-gallon milk pails like this one, and sunk into well water to keep the milk below 60 degrees.

But now, to continue to sell their milk, they had to chill it to below 50 degrees—impossible without big metal cooling tanks. The legislature stepped in and reached a compromise with the milk regulators on that—but there was still one more problem. Milk collected in the 10-gallon pails could not be sold as Grade A (drinking milk), and there was no local market for Grade B (cheese milk).

The local Amish dairy farmers, who at that time still didn't have access to electrical power, were facing financial ruin.

Enter local Amish farmer Ralph Bontrager.

Ralph had a vision. He thought that there should be a cheese making facility right in the heart of Amish Indiana that could take all that Grade B milk and make it into quality cheese to sell both wholesale and, eventually, in a retail store on-site. But how to finance it?

Ralph approached the management team at Jayco, the first of many RV companies to build a manufacturing plant in the area. He asked them to consider financing a cheese making plant.

As you can imagine, it was a hard sell—but eventually, they said yes. An article from the South Bend Tribune (Jan 4 1992) quotes the then-Jayco-president Allen Yoder as saying, "It was a year before we acted. Ralph had a hard time selling us on the idea." But Jayco founder Lloyd Bontrager realized that the survival of the Amish economy was at risk. Allen Yoder continued in the article, "We had enough to do at our factory without running a cheese plant. We told Ralph, 'We will do it, but you will have to manage it.'"

And so the plant was built, and it opened in 1979—with three Jayco executives as the owners (Lloyd Bontrager, Allen Yoder, and Larry Schrock) and Ralph Bontrager (who lived next to the factory) as the general manager. The work force in those days consisted of Ralph's family, two other employees, and a professional cheese maker from Berlin, Ohio. On its first day of operation, the company website says, the plant received one can milk truck containing about 15,000 pounds of milk.

Since that day, the plant has grown steadily and gone through two changes in ownership (with corresponding name changes). Their website says they process 400,000 pounds of milk per day into 40,000 pounds of longhorn and deli horn cheeses.

Heritage Ridge Creamery sells cheese they make on-site (as well as other products) in their retail shop on the premises from Monday through Saturday, 9 to 4. Specialties include Colby, Cheddar, Colby Jack, Pepper Jack, and other stirred-curd cheeses. On weekday mornings you can often watch the cheese being made through long glass windows on the back wall of the store. It's shipped all over the country under various labels. They also have a retail website.

Ralph still lives nearby, and it's been quite a while since he worked in the dairy industry, but his legacy lives on at "The Cheese House."

Galen and Cora: Starting Over

Years ago I attended the wedding of a young Amish couple—we'll
call them Galen and Cora. I watched as the young couple began their
lives in Amish Indiana. Galen took over the family farm. He was a
bright young man, and out in the barn, he began a business of his own
making lawn furniture—at first from wood, and then plastic lumber,
which was a new trend at that time.

The business grew, and soon he was employing his father, brothers,
and cousins. When I had a tour of the business around 2008, he was
selling to retailers all over the country and was on the verge of a
contract with a local university to make special furniture for their
sports training room (in the school colors!). Business was booming.

The next time I visited, Cora's mother told me that Galen and Cora
were leaving it all and moving to southern Michigan. Their new farm
would be about 17 miles away—a long distance in their culture,
considering that a horse and buggy aren't good for a trip that long.
Cora wasn't thrilled with the decision, as she was leaving everything

she'd ever known to be a newcomer in an Amish settlement unfamiliar to her. But there had been Amish in southern Michigan for generations; in fact, Galen's ancestors had lived there before coming to Indiana.

Later that year I visited their new farm in Michigan. They owned eight acres with house and outbuildings and were renting one hundred more. They hoped to make a go of it as dairy farmers. The house and barns were in bad shape and needed lots of work! In the winter they slept on the living room floor, gathered around a potbelly stove.

Some time later I asked Cora's mother, why would Galen leave his thriving business and family farm to move to such a relatively faraway place and start over? She said, "I don't know… I think it was all just too much for him." Recently I talked to Galen about it, and he said, "The furniture business involved a lot of paperwork. Whenever I could get away from that and be outdoors or doing the farm chores, I felt so much happier. I could see that as the business grew, it was going to be more and more paperwork, so I decided to make a change."

One interesting thing: The farm had been owned by an English farmer, so it was wired for electricity. Amish families who move into homes with electricity are allowed to use it for one year, by which time it has to be removed. Cora remarked at one point, "I sure will miss that dishwasher!"

Once in a while I like to grab some fresh baked goods and head up there to visit them, and sometimes I bring Cora's parents along. Galen and Cora don't get a lot of visitors from home, since normally it involves hiring a driver to make the trip. Amazingly, although a horse and buggy cannot make the trip, Cora's parents, who are in their late fifties as I write this, regularly make the round trip (seventeen miles each way) on their bicycles!

It's 2014 as I write this, and Galen and Cora have seven children. They are making a go of it in Michigan. Gradually they are fixing up their house and outbuildings and making a life there—and they have a fine new stove which heats the entire house! At first, during the winter, Galen had to take a job in a recreational vehicle factory to make ends meet, leaving Cora to run the farm during the day. But before long their dairy herd increased, and they were able to purchase the 100 acres they had been renting, adjacent to their farm. Presently they are milking 50 cows, and they have passed the three-year prep period beyond which they can sell their milk as "organic," meaning more income. Their two oldest boys are now big enough to help out. Soon Galen will purchase more land across the road; he needs to grow more corn to feed his herd.

Witnessing their struggles and their courage reminds me of the stories of my pioneer ancestors on the Nebraska prairie. I admire Galen and Cora, and I'm glad I've been able to watch their story as it unfolds.

Postscript: It is now 2023, and my friends have eight children and a thriving farm in Michigan. It's still one of my favorite places to visit!

Remembering Rudy

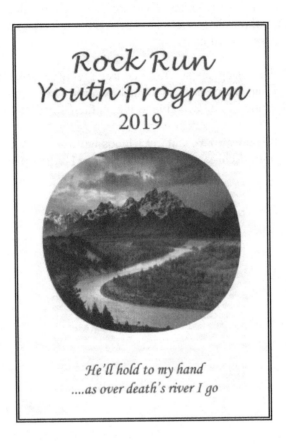

Rock Run
Youth Program
2019

He'll hold to my hand
....as over death's river I go

As I write this in late 2019, last night I went to a performance put on by the Rock Run Amish Youth Program. When I say "youth," I mean Amish young people between the ages of sixteen and marriage, which can often be mid- or late twenties. There are several Amish youth centers in the area—the Cove in Shipshewana and Rock Run near Millersburg are two of them. They sponsor all kinds of activities and sports leagues for the local Amish youth.

Anyway, last night was the first performance and it was "family night." There will be four more performances for non-family members who are lucky enough to get tickets, on upcoming Friday and Saturday evenings.

So there I was, with three or four hundred family members of the performers—one of only a handful of English people in the large pole barn at the youth center. My young friend Jay was one of the youth involved in the program, and I was sitting with a dozen of his family members, ages infant to eighty.

I've been to a few of these youth concerts before, but this one was special.

Backtracking a bit:
Last May, there was a terrible accident in Amish Indiana. A young man named Rudy (names changed) was riding his bike home from an evening with his friends when he was killed by a drunk driver. The driver was his childhood friend, an Amish kid gone wild. (Perhaps I'll write about that another time—that story is still evolving.) The visitation and funeral lasted two full days and brought together many, many hundreds of Rudy's friends and family.

It's been a hard summer for all of Rudy's friends, including his best friend Jay. They have spent nearly every Saturday night at Rudy's parents' home. In Amish Indiana, friends become like family. And Rudy had been one of the youth participating in the Rock Run music program this year.

So, back to last night:
I found myself at the program, and it was lovely. There were plays and songs, lasting almost 2½ hours—some humorous, some serious. The theme on the cover doesn't seem so depressing when you consider what was in the kids' minds and hearts—Rudy, their absent friend.

Each performer's name was also listed in the program, along with the names of their parents—typical of the close family ties in this community. First on the list was Rudy. His parents and a dozen other relatives sat together, the women in their black dresses of mourning, two rows in front of us. A side table held a beautiful bouquet of red roses—one for each youth in the program, and one white rose, for Rudy.

At one point late in the concert, the young performers sang a song that was particularly meaningful to Rudy. As they sang it, each one held a lit candle. After the song, they silently filed down the side stairs of the stage and placed their lit candles on the table in front of the roses. There were tears in a lot of eyes, including mine. But it was a wonderful way for his friends to honor Rudy's memory.

Shopping Misadventures with Rebecca

FOR AN AVERAGE WEDDING YOU WILL NEED...
- Approximately 1,200-1,500 napkins (50 napkins in each pack)
- About 3 rolls table covers (each roll is 100')

***The 250ft rolls (white & ivory) are thinner & recommended to use to cover tables, not as table cloths

When we used to visit Amish Indiana as tourists, we would often run errands with our Amish friends. It saved them time, and it was a good excuse to socialize. It also got me into lots of Amish homes and businesses I would never have had access to on my own. But one favorite shopping stop of the local Amish is the Walmart in Goshen. It's the nearest "big box store" to the Shipshewana-Lagrange County Amish settlement. And on the same road in Goshen is a Menard's and an Aldi's that they also like to patronize—as my husband calls them, the Amish Shopping Trifecta. One time my friend Rebecca and I were shopping at the Aldi's and we had a couple of tense moments.

Rebecca is a very organized person, so she has been asked multiple times to be in charge of the food for the Amish wedding of one or another of her nieces. This is a huge responsibility. Special kitchen trailers are rented that have banks of stoves and ovens and refrigerators in them to handle the massive amounts of food that are prepared, with about 1,000 meals served by the end of the day.

So Rebecca was buying large quantities of certain non-perishable items in advance, and I came along with my Jeep to lend a hand. She had planned very carefully what she would buy that day and what it would cost. By the time she made the rounds, we each had a cartful of food. One thing she bought was 50 packets of powdered salad dressing mix. And while she was there, Rebecca was picking up a jumbo economy pack of diapers for one of her married daughters.

As we stood in the checkout line, the clerk said to Rebecca, "So you're planning a wedding?" But at the very moment Rebecca was answering "Yes, we are!" to that question, she was also heaving the gigantic pack of diapers up onto the conveyor belt. It was an awkward moment, as it really looked like the diapers were being bought for the bride! (I've been asked more than once to re-enact that little moment for the amusement of my Amish friends, since I tell the story more dramatically than Rebecca does.)

So... We finished checking out and the clerk told Rebecca the total—around $400, as I recall. Rebecca's face turned really pale and she whispered to me, "That's not what I figured at all—I don't have that much money!" So we stalled the clerk for a minute while we frantically tried to figure out what to do. My Visa card was no good, since Aldi's doesn't take credit cards. I didn't have a debit card, and neither did she. Neither did I have my checkbook on me, nor enough cash to cover the shortfall. What to do?

As we brainstormed, the clerk suddenly exclaimed, "Oops, wait! I'm so sorry! I charged you for 500 packets of salad dressing mix instead of 50 packets!" So the clerk made the correction; the color returned to Rebecca's face; she paid for the purchases; and we were on our way back home. Whew.

Out of the Doghouse: A Mother's Day Surprise

As I write this (May 2013), Gary and I just got back from two days in Amish Indiana. As usual, it was filled with good food, beautiful scenery, time with Amish friends, and lots of R&R.

It's a tradition that my Amish friend Rebecca and I go to one of the local Amish-owned greenhouses in May to get our spring annuals— we've done it probably half a dozen times now. My friends' two youngest boys were old enough to handle the milking by themselves this year, so her husband Gerald went with us to the greenhouse.

Later that Friday afternoon, the four of us made a few other stops (business and pleasure) and then headed out to eat supper together. The subject of Mother's Day came up as we drove. Gerald looked very surprised as he said, "What? Mother's Day is this weekend?" Rebecca (she and I sit in the back seat and talk while the men ride up front) looked at me with an expression that said, "Guess who forgot to get me something for Mother's Day?" We could see that Gerald was in the doghouse.

The next morning (Saturday) I got an early phone call. We had mistakenly left a flat of Rebecca's "Wave Petunias" in the back of our Jeep after the greenhouse run the previous day, which gave Gerald the perfect chance to volunteer to walk to their phone shanty and call us. He said, "Are you going to be near the greenhouse today? Remember that orange rose that Rebecca admired there? I left some money in the workshop, clipped to my tape measure. We'll be gone this morning. Could you take the money, get that rose for Rebecca, and put it in the workshop? It would be nice to surprise her with it on Mother's Day tomorrow."

We were glad to help. I did remember the rose she admired, so Gary and I picked it up, brought it out to the farm, left it in the shed, and took the money. This is one Amishman who is going to be out of the doghouse on Mother's Day after all!

Shaklee Chris

Recently (it's 2013 as I write this), I took this photo on the road in front of a certain Amishman's farmhouse near Shipshewana, Indiana. That Amishman could only be "Shaklee Chris."

Chris was born in an Amish community in Kansas, but has lived his adult life in Lagrange County, Indiana, where he has eight children, all of whom remained Amish. One of his sons runs the farm now, and Shaklee Chris lives in the "Dawdi Haus" across the driveway

Chris is in his mid-eighties as I write this, and for many years he has been an enthusiastic distributor/dealer of Shaklee products. Once a week for many years, he has had a driver take him on his rounds, picking up Shaklee products and then delivering them all over the countryside.

Chris is a very good Shaklee dealer. Quite a few years back, he received a letter inviting him to attend the annual Shaklee convention in California. He didn't take the letter seriously, he told me; besides, California is a long way from Indiana by train, and the Amish don't fly. But after a few more letters, he asked his Shaklee supervisor about it, who assured him that his sales numbers were so high that he qualified to attend.

Once there, he discovered that his sales were high enough to qualify for a car! (A program in existence at that time for the top Shaklee distributors in each region.) Obviously he had no use for a car… so Shaklee made him a special deal. They told him to select and purchase a brand-new buggy and a buggy horse, and send them the bill.

Over the years Shaklee Chris won a horse and buggy eight times. Each time he passed it on to one of his grandsons who was turning sixteen. I can only imagine the publicity that Shaklee got from this! But Chris tells the story with amusement and pride. This is one special Amishman—and as of this writing (2013), he still sells Shaklee.

Shaklee Chris Goes to the Car Show

My husband Gary recently traveled from our home in Illinois to meet some old friends at a hot rod event in Ohio, and he decided to break his journey in Amish Indiana, where he could have some great pie and stay at one of our favorite B&Bs.

His stop was over a Thursday night, so he decided to go to the cruise-in that happens at Essenhaus Inn in Middlebury on Thursday evenings in the summer. A "cruise-in," for those of you not married to a "gearhead," is when owners of old cars show up at a designated place and spend the evening checking out each other's cars. Sometimes there is music, food, and/or trophies. Lots of spectators show up at the bigger cruise-ins, and the event at Essenhaus is huge.

I remarked that Shaklee Chris, one of our older Amish friends, had been wanting to attend the cruise-in some time, but it was too far by buggy and his adult children didn't want him to ride his bike there alone! (He is 85.) My husband Gary left a voice mail for Chris, and soon it was arranged.

Gary arrived in Amish Indiana and picked up Chris. They headed to Essenhaus, where Chris treated Gary to dinner. Then they spent some time wandering up and down the rows of old cars. My husband said that Chris was the only Amishman he saw there.

Later, on the way back to Shipshewana from Middlebury, Chris told Gary some inside stories about the local Amish—and about some of the local business owners who were now English but had grown up Amish. They made a couple of stops, including an Amish buggy shop run by one of Chris' grandsons. He makes a good living making buggies for the locals, and he picks up extra money from an arrangement that a tour company made with him. They stop by with busloads of tourists who want to look around his buggy shop, and he gets paid a fee. He said he often sees two groups a week.

I was glad to see my husband so comfortable with the Amish. It was his first trip into their world without me, and he passed the test with flying colors!

Postscript - Shaklee Chris passed away on April 5, 2017.

Melinda

I met the most delightful child the other day.

It happened at my friend Rose's lovely Amish farmhouse, where Rose's elderly mother, my friend Mrs. R, was staying for a few weeks. Rose's granddaughter Melinda, age seven and in first grade, had heard I was coming and she was waiting for me. She likes music and wanted to be there.

As I opened my hymnal and started picking out songs to sing, Melinda began to hover closer, and soon she was looking over my shoulder. I pulled up a chair and she gladly sat down. As I held the songbook so she could see it, I could see her eyes following my finger, and soon she was mouthing the words as I sang them—no small feat for a first grader, who had probably never seen a regular music score before, and for whom English was her second language! I was amazed she could follow the lines of words from verse to verse, but she could.

So I stopped a few times and explained how music scores work... I told her that when the notes go up on the page, my voice would go up. Later I explained that the hollow notes were held longer than the solid black ones, and I demonstrated that.

She sat for three quarters of an hour, enthralled, following the songs as I sang them and often mouthing the words. I told her that when she got older, there was a group of Amish young people locally who meet every winter for ten or twelve weeks, learning to read sheet music and singing hymns in four-part harmony. She thought that sounded wonderful.

A week went by, and I was back at Rose's house singing to Mrs. R. again. As I walked in, the two of them were gazing out the window, across the open fields behind the farmhouse. There was young Melinda, riding her pony across the fields, flying like the wind, with all the skill of a little cowgirl. It was amazing!

Rose shouted that I was there to sing to her great-grandma, and Melinda quickly put the pony away and came across the fields, holding something. It was for me.

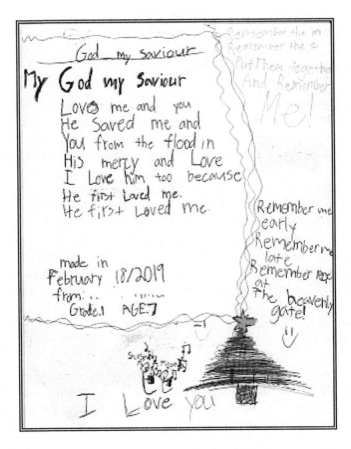

Melinda had written a song the previous Sunday afternoon after church, and she wanted me to have it. (I have concealed her name, but the rest is just as she drew it.) She sang the song to me and gave me the drawing. I told her it would go right up on my refrigerator when I got home—and it did!

More about Melinda in a later chapter.

Jonas Stutzman, Amish Eccentric

It's always fun to find a person of historical interest in a family tree, and even more fun to find a "colorful character." When I decided to do some genealogy for my original Amish friends, I found a man who was both.

These particular Amish friends have a history in Lagrange County, Indiana that goes back about six generations. Like most Northern Indiana Amish, their roots trace back mostly to Holmes County, Ohio— which is presently the largest Amish settlement in the world, numbering around 60,000.

But someone had to be the first Amishman to go west from Pennsylvania and settle in Holmes County, Ohio—and it happens that he was an ancestor of my Amish friends. His name was Jonas Stutzman, but he was known in his later life as "White Jonas" ("Der Weiss" in German). Much has been written about him.

Jonas Stutzman (1788-1871) was born in Pennsylvania and came to Ohio in 1809, where he married Magdalena Gerber and had at least nine children. The 1850 census finds him in Walnut Creek, aged 62, living with second wife Catherine and the youngest four of his eight surviving children. According to the German Cultural Museum there, Jonas built the area's first sawmill and the area's first schoolhouse.

In 1850 he published a booklet in which he claimed that God had revealed to him in a vision that "the time of the fulfillment of his plan with mankind is at hand." He said that Christ's second coming would be in 1853. So sure was Jonas of this fact, and so sure that he would meet Christ personally upon his return to earth, that he built a special chair for Jesus to sit in when he arrived! (The chair is in the local museum today.)

Jonas had other visions. It was revealed to him, so he said, that the children of God should wear only beige, gray, and white—"the colors of eagles and sheep." Even after 1853 came and went with no sign of Christ's second coming, he wore only white for the rest of his life.

Steven Nolt, in his book A History of the Amish, says that although the Amish church rejected his teachings, "White Jonas" Stutzman remained a member in good standing. "His peculiar views and dress were not seen as a threat to anyone, for he never had any followers." The census records show that Jonas lived the rest of his life peacefully in Holmes County, residing with his son Daniel in his old age.

ALL GOD'S CREATURES

Making a Bid, or Swatting a Fly?

When we used to visit Amish Indiana, it was often for a long weekend. If I was there on a Friday morning, any time of year, I liked to watch the horse auction. The Shipshewana Auction building is on the main north-south street in town (State Route 5). Every Friday, year round, is horse auction day.

You enter the auction pit from the upper level, and below are wooden platforms and a few scattered chairs. The first thing you notice is the smell! Horse auctions are not for the squeamish—it does smell like a barn. The crowd is mostly male and about half Amish, half English on a typical Friday morning.

I learned how easy it is to place a bid one morning when I swatted at a fly and saw the auctioneer point at me and take my "bid." I frantically started motioning "No! No!" and the auctioneer just laughed and remarked (over the microphone), "Looks like the lady was just swatting a fly!" Tack (harnesses, etc.) is auctioned off first, and then later in the morning it's the horses—the big draft horses, the relatively smaller buggy horses, and the ponies.

Most of the draft horses used for field work are Belgians. They are huge animals, some of the larger ones approaching two thousand pounds, but very gentle. I asked an Amish friend one time—Why Belgians instead of Clydesdales? He said, "We like the way the

Belgians look." Percherons are occasionally used here; I saw a Percheron wall calendar in the kitchen of one Amishman who prefers that breed.

The buggy horses are mostly Standardbred horses and mostly brown. I was surprised to learn that many of them come from Canada. Racehorses that are not fast enough to compete on the race track may end up going south to Indiana and becoming Amish buggy horses. Horseback riding is rare here, though, and mostly a hobby of the young people.

Ponies are common on the farms and are used with little pony carts. It's a great way for Amish children to learn the horse-and-buggy skills they will need as adults. It can also be their transportation to and from school. My niece Bee used to love riding around in a pony cart with the children of my Amish friends.

Anyway, getting back to the horse auction:

The main entrance is on the south side, and there is a sign there that says "no photographs." This is because of the many Amishmen who attend the auction. But I stopped by after the auction one day and asked if I could take a picture of the auction pit, and the auctioneers had no problem with that.

I never get tired of sitting in the stands and watching the beautiful animals brought in and auctioned off. Maybe it's not a typical tourist activity, but it's real life in My Amish Indiana.

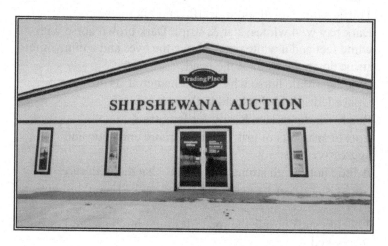

Upheaded and Ready for the Miles

----------------------------(7x) > 3/15/18----------------------------------

For Sale: Cheyenne rei **GELDING**. TSS, stands to hitch and at corners, woman driver, been to church and town, all trot, $4500. Wayne Miller, 0725N 600W, LaGrange, IN.

----------------------------(4x) > 2/15/18----------------------------

I love looking through the classified ads in "The People's Exchange," a local biweekly Amish-centric publication. My favorite is the horses-for-sale section. But what does all these terms mean? I decided to find out.

Below is a list of terms I often see in these ads. I talked to a couple of Amish friends to find out what they mean...

- TSS: Traffic safe and sound
- Stands to hitch and at corners: It'll stop and stay until you tell it to go
- Woman driver: Very well trained
- Been to church and town: It's well trained and safe anywhere you take it
- All trot: Trotting means front and back legs work diagonally – steadier
- All pace: Pacing means two left legs step, then two right legs – faster
- Traffic safe: Not afraid of traffic and big trucks
- Dark bay w/ 4 whites, star & strip: Dark brown horse with white feet and a white patch above the eyes and a thin white stripe down the front of the head
- Gelding: Male horse who's been neutered, as 90% are
- Upheaded: Holds his head high
- Ready for the miles: Ready for long trips
- Lots of snap/lots of grit: A faster, more energetic and aggressive horse
- A little hot: High strung; may balk – handle with care
- Sticky starter: A balker. (My friend said, "I wouldn't buy it!")
- Watches stuff beside the road: It might lurch out into traffic if spooked

- Chunky: More muscular
- Needs miles: Needs to be used regularly to continue and maintain training
- Average 10 mph: This is a bit slow; 12 mph is better
- Nice big stretch mare, drives w/ tight lines: Hang onto her – she wants to go fast!
- Broodmare only: Too old to do work (or never trained to)
- Boys' horse: Faster and more energetic and perhaps not as well trained
- Safe for dawdi and school kids: Very well trained; very safe; probably very slow too
- Babysitter pony: Very tame and good around kids
- Would make good produce team: Draft horses which are well trained for a wagon

I was surprised to learn that horses don't begin their training for the buggy or plow until they are two years old! There are various levels of training, or "broke" as they call it:

- Not broke: Very young with no training
- Green broke: 2-3 years old; trained well enough to pull a buggy
- Good/well broke: Typically 5 years old; most anyone could drive it
- Broke for women: Very well trained, and expensive to buy. Not the fastest, though
- Broke for anybody or dead broke: A "dawdi horse"—good for the elderly
- Broke, broke, broke: A very slow horse!
- Good broke to ride, green to drive: A riding horse that learned to pull a buggy later
- Broke to all machinery: A draft horse, usually a Belgian but perhaps a Percheron

I saw some other phrases in this week's ads that I liked… How about this one? "Skittish in the barn, but get him out on the road, he'll go all day, no problem."

So the next time you see an ad that says, "Dark bay w/ 4 whites, star, & strip," you'll know what that means!

High Steppers

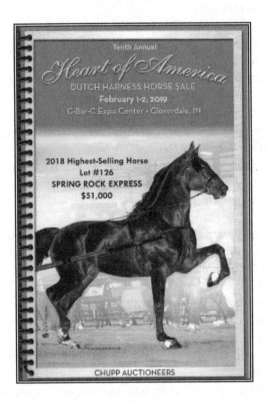

A few years back my Amish friend Emmon and his wife Lily made a request to Gary… They and some other horse-loving friends wanted to make their annual trip to Cloverdale, Indiana for the Dutch Harness Horse auction. Would Gary rent a 14-passenger van and drive them, if they paid for the van, the fuel, and our motel room? I'm always up for an auction of any kind, and my husband had nothing else planned—so off we went.

This particular auction draws buyers from all over the Midwest for those who like the Dutch Harness breed. According to Wikipedia, "The Dutch Harness Horse is a fine driving horse that has been developed in the Netherlands since the end of World War II." It goes on to say this: "With 40 sires and fewer than 2,000 broodmares the population is not large, and Dutch Harness Horses are highly recognizable." Wikipedia also explained why they have a distinctive, high-stepping trot: "The forelegs are typically longer than the hind

74

legs… and as such the horse will 'sink' in the back and rise in the front. This quality is responsible for the powerful, active hind end and the great freedom in the forehand."

Not every Amishman is a Dutch Harness fan, though. I was told that many think they aren't as good for the miles as the more common Standardbreds. Lily said that people say Dutch Harness Horses are "all show and no go!" Others think they're stubborn and distractible, a bit hard to control, and have "poor brakes" unless trained very carefully. For that reason, many of the horses in this sale were half Dutch and half Standardbred.

But I don't go to auctions just for the auction! I like to do plenty of people-watching. As an Englisher I was in the minority at this event; probably 98% of those around me were Amish. In addition to the northern Indiana Amish I see nearly every day, there were Amish from Iowa, Ohio, Kentucky, and my favorite—Lancaster County, Pennsylvania. I love to observe the differences. I asked Emmon, "Of all the people in this arena, how many do you know by name?" and he said, "almost all of them." Unlike me, Emmon is an extrovert to the core.

But there was an auction going on, too! I can listen to horse auctioneers for hours... Their descriptions the horses always make me smile. This time I heard phrases like these: "A kitten in the barn but a tiger on the road!" and "A boys' horse deluxe with a lot of power!" and "He will look just as good pulling your buggy to church as he will in the show ring!"

The names of the horses amuse me, too. They ranged from the traditional, like "Class Act" and "Firecracker," to the more creative, like "Susquehanna County," "I'm a Good Girl," and "Mass Psychology."

One of the superstar stud horses in the Dutch Harness world is named "Winston." He had a two-page full color spread in the auction catalog. I heard his name at least a hundred times in two days! A few dozen of his offspring were for sale, and they brought the best prices at the sale. Three breeding shares were auctioned off (the chance to breed one mare a year to Winston for his lifetime) and they sold for $8,000 to $10,000 apiece!

Emmon, who is a diehard horse guy, told me on the way home that one of his mares is a Winston offspring. He also told me why Winston isn't pictured in his two-page spread, but rather a couple of his champion offspring. The reason? Although Winston's offspring are gorgeous animals, Emmon said that Winston himself is, as my dad would say, "homely as a mud fence"!

The horses really were amazing. Many were "bay" (very dark brown) or black, not the medium-brown color of the Standardbreds usually seen in my part of Indiana. And with their heads held high and their high-stepping motion, they were a pleasure to watch. Thanks for including us on this trip, Emmon and Lily!

P.S. This group of Amish horse fans travel together regularly, and they have developed a diabolical tradition. Lily told me that I should save my trash after our DQ stop. Why? Because whoever gets dropped off first (and it took an hour to drop everyone off)—they get everybody's trash dropped onto their driveway! And people didn't make it easy for them; some of the DQ bags were tossed into a puddle! Seems like a fair trade, though, for getting to bed an hour earlier after a long day.

Losing a Good Horse

One time years ago when I was visiting Amish Indiana, I drove my friend Rebecca to Menard's in Goshen to buy a vacuum cleaner. Since she'd never bought one before, she was glad for my input! The Amish don't have a lot of carpets—they like linoleum the best—but a few families will share a vacuum cleaner for those times when it's needed. (Note: They typically plug a vacuum into a gas-powered generator.)

What does this have to do with losing a good horse, you may wonder?

I was using my husband's pickup truck, which I've driven only a few times. He's very fond of it, and he doesn't even like dust on it, so he rarely allows it out of his sight! As we parked at the far end of the lot as I had promised to do, I explained to Rebecca that Gary is very fond of this truck and likes it parked out in the boondocks; I showed her the "pinstripes" that he had hired someone to paint on it.

She remarked that her husband Gerald was similarly fond of their main buggy horse. He had raised the horse himself, and she said he once remarked, "I wouldn't take $5,000 for this horse." (Typical prices at that time were half that much.) Whenever one of their children needed a buggy horse, Gerald always held that one back if he could, and sent them out with a different one.

But a few weeks prior, Gerald's special horse (not the one in the picture) had died from West Nile Virus. The horse was only four years old—the prime of life for a buggy horse. She said her husband didn't usually get emotional about animals, but this had been a hard thing for him to take.

They had noticed the previous Friday that the horse seemed lame in one back leg. By Sunday they realized something was very wrong, and they suspected West Nile Virus, which had killed a few other horses in the area. First thing Monday morning Gerald phoned the veterinarian, but she didn't show up right away. He called four times that day, asking her to come as soon as she could. By the time she arrived, at 8:00 in the evening, it was too late, and the horse was too far gone. Rebecca said that Gerald couldn't stop wondering whether his favorite horse could have been saved if the vet had arrived sooner.

There is a vaccine for horses which prevents West Nile Virus, but it's very expensive. The vet said the best thing to do is to keep the horses pastured as far as possible away from the woods. At any rate, it was too late for Gerald's favorite horse, and that made me sad.

Sheep in Shipshe—a New Thing

There's an increasing number of sheep to be seen on the local hillsides around here, which is something new. One of my good friends here recently began raising sheep, so I paid him a visit last week to find out more. Last fall he purchased 80 ewes, and now (it's May 2022 as I write this) it's lambing time!

Steve's ewes (female adults) are a cross breed—they are half Katahdin and half Dorper. He also has a couple of Katahdin rams as a part of his herd.

I never knew (until now) that there are two distinct categories of sheep. There are those raised for their wool, of course—but there are also those raised for their meat, commonly called "hair sheep." Steve's Katahdins and Dorpers are breeds of hair sheep. They still grow a thicker coat in the winter, and they shed it in the spring, like most outdoor animals. But they don't need to be sheared, nor is their coat a good source of wool. They were bred for their ability to produce high quality lamb or mutton meat.

The ewes can produce offspring about every eight months, and the babies take five months to gestate. The ewes can breed any time of year—but Steve separates the rams from the herd in July so he won't have any lambs born in the winter.

Steve told me that sheep are notorious for getting sick and dying so quickly that nothing can be done for them. For that reason, sheep farmers say, "A sick sheep is a dead sheep."

Of the 80 females Steve purchased last fall, 76 remained this spring to have offspring, and about 50 have given birth so far. Typically this type of ewe can have two or three lambs, but Steve's herd are all first-time mothers, so one lamb apiece is the norm. A few of them did have twins—and in the case of the two surviving sets of twins, Steve took the stronger lamb of each pair and brought it to his daughter's farm, where they are being bottle-fed—something that Steve's three young grandchildren are enjoying very much! Other strategies for motherless lambs: Sometimes a mother without a lamb can be convinced to "adopt" a lamb without a mother. And Steve's young neighbor Jay put a motherless lamb together with a mama goat with great success!

A full-grown sheep of this type weighs around 100-110 pounds, but he sells the lambs when they reach ideal weight for lamb meat, which is about 60 pounds. But all his female lambs for this year are already reserved for a fellow Amishman, who is going to use them as ewes to start his own herd.

Steve told me there are somewhere between 100 and 200 local Amish farmers raising sheep now—six in his church district alone. He said that the typical herd size depends on acreage of pasture available, since a sheep farmer can have five to eight ewes per acre. In Steve's case, he has plenty of land. He has four or five pastures which he alternates; he says that it's best to move the herd when they eat the grass down very low, because the pests and parasites are mostly found close to the ground. His pastures are bordered by an electric fence wire about knee-high—that's all it takes to keep the sheep contained—although he has regular fencing around the perimeters of his land.

Likes and dislikes of sheep? Steve told me that the sheep really like hills, so they love to run up and down the small hilly areas on his land. What they dislike is wet feet, so they stay out of the water.

Next time you're in the area, maybe you'll notice the number of sheep dotting the pastures. The Amish culture may be slow to embrace change, but not everything stays the same forever around here!

Velcro

It's early spring 2020, and I haven't written anything in a while. I usually write in the winter months after Christmas—but this year, that time slot was taken up by Velcro. No, not Velcro the trademarked hook-and-loop closure—Velcro the puppy.

My husband and I have never been dog people (or pet people of any kind). All four of our parents grew up as farm kids, and none of them would ever have thought of having "animals in the house," so both Gary and I grew up with the same attitude. One of our unofficial vows when we got married in 2007 was "No pets."

But… we moved from suburban Chicago to Middlebury, Indiana—My Amish Indiana, as I call it—when we retired in 2017. Before long I wanted to make some extra "pin money" for my new shade garden, so I started to drive for a few Amish friends. One of them was Ennis and his wife Lily, who had a very nice kennel and raised poodles, Aussiedoodles, and goldendoodles. (No, not a puppy mill! Don't get me started...)

So a couple of years went by, and I really got to like the little poodle and doodle puppies. I would stop by their kennel at least once a week, just to cuddle the puppies. (I called myself their "Vice President of Socialization.") I told my friends, "I still don't like dogs! But I like puppies."

Sometimes a puppy came along that I especially liked. One of those was Coop, a black goldendoodle pup who was so affectionate that I nicknamed him "Velcro" because he really liked to lean on my shoulder! He was the smallest of his litter and rather shy, but very sweet.

Then last Christmas week, something terrible happened... Coop, age four months by then, broke his front leg playing outside. I drove Ennis and little Coop to the vet, and after the pup was sedated and the leg was set and splinted, the vet brought him back out to the car. The vet said that Coop needed to be in a quiet place for four to six weeks, away from other dogs. Ennis had a couple new litters at that time and he was the busiest he'd ever been—so I said, "Maybe I could take Coop home until his leg gets better, if Gary doesn't mind." Ennis immediately took up my offer!

To my great surprise, my husband agreed to this plan, and I took Coop home that very day. At first Gary referred to the little pup as "that darn thing"—but right around week three, I came home one night to find my husband curled up in the easy chair with Coop, and I could hear him saying, "Who's a good dog? You're a good dog!" Busted! The walls of resistance were coming down.

By the time Coop's splint was about to come off, we were both pretty smitten with the little guy—first I was, and then Gary... and having a dog in the house was easier than we thought. I used to make fun of people who "loved" their dogs and treated them like people, but now I was having to eat my own words! I was starting to think about keeping him, but what about my significant other?

One Monday morning soon after, as I headed to the kennel for a vet run with Ennis, my husband said, "This morning I ordered Velcro a proper dog bed." And then the next day, Gary said to me, "Ask Ennis how much he wants for the dog."

82

And so, Coop (now renamed Velcro) came home to live with a couple of sixty-somethings who thought they didn't like dogs!... His leg has healed well, and now our house would be so different without his sweet little face! He has brought us lots of joy, and I think he likes living with us too!

Melinda's Puppy: A Guest Post

> Puppy Love
>
> One day I was reading the "Peoples Exchange. Wanting to buy a maltese or toy poodle. Finely I found a multypoo for sale in the back of the Peoples, for $600.00.
>
> My siblings and I decided to put all our money together. Hannah (age 9) had $251.21, Caleb (age 7) had $11.07, Benji (age 5) had $10.02, Elam (age 3) had $3.00, I (age 11) had $289.42. So our total came out to $564.70.
>
> Oh no! I called people who owned the puppy and told them I wanted the puppy very much, but had only $546.70 without thinking and being a little nervous. At the time it was almost dark I went to bed and then it crossed my mind that I had told her $546.70 instead of $564.70. So early the next morning I called her and told her I actually had $564.70.
>
> On Tuesday morning she called back and told me I could have the puppy for $564. I called the owner and told her we would pick up the puppy the next day at 1:30 pm.
>
> So the next day my aunt Katherine took me to get the puppy. When we got there the owners told us that 15 min. before we got

I have special treat for you! This is a guest post by "Melinda," a young lady I've written about before. She is now eleven years old, and she's quite a writer already—especially considering that English is her second language! Here's how it happened:

I was having lunch at Das Kaffee Haus in Shipshewana the other day with Melinda, her younger sister, and their grandmother Rose, a good friend of mine.

Melinda was telling me about their new puppy, and her enthusiasm was contagious. I asked her, "Could you write out this story so I can publish it on my website?" That very same evening I got a call from her saying that her story was already done—along with a second one about her pony.

So here it is, just as she wrote it except for a few spelling corrections and name changes—and thank you, Melinda!

* * * * * * * * * * * * * * * *

Puppy Love

One day I was reading The People's Exchange, wanting to buy a Maltese or toy poodle. Finally I found a Maltipoo for sale in the back of the People's, for $600.

My siblings and I decided to put all our money together. Holly (age 9) had $251.21; Caleb (age 7) had $11.07; Ben (age 5) had $10.02; Eli (age 3) had $3.00; I (age 11) had $289.49. So our total came out to $564.70.

Oh, no! I called the people who owned the puppy and told them I wanted the puppy very much but had only $546.70, without thinking and being a little nervous. At the time it was almost dark. I went to bed and then it crossed my mind that I had told her $546.70 instead of $564.70! So early the next morning I called her and told her I actually had $564.70.

On Tuesday morning she called back and told me I could have the puppy for $564. I called the owner and told her we would pick up the puppy the next day at 1:30 p.m.

So the next day my aunt Katherine took me to get the puppy. When we got there the owners told us that 15 minutes before we got there another woman had come there to buy the puppy. The owners of the puppy told the lady that they had sold the puppy to me already.

We named the puppy Zenny.
We are now having a very
very lot of fun with Zenny. :)

With Love,
Melinda and Holly
11/15/22

Melinda's Pony: Another Guest Post

Here's a second guest post from young Melinda. I recently asked her to write up the story of her new puppy, and when she gave it to me, she also gave me the story of her beloved pony! Melinda is quite a horsewoman for an eleven-year-old—a natural-born rider. So here's her pony story...

* * * * * * * * * * * * * * * *

Pony Love

One day when I was seven years old, my family and I went to a pony auction at the MEC [the Michiana Events Center].
We went up the stairs and onto the second floor. Then we found some empty chairs.

Mom, Holly, my brothers, and I had to use the restroom. So we went down to the first floor. I was done using the restroom before the others were.

So I went up the stairs to sit by my father. When I got there I saw this beautiful brown and white pony come into the ring. I told my father I wanted that pony! He asked me if I was sure, because he had just gotten a brown one. I told him I was sure and that I had always wanted a brown and white pony. He then told me that I would get the pony if I would take care of him. I told him I would. So he got the pony for me.

I named the pony Teddy. I love him very very much.

He loves barrel racing, monkey-in-a-tree, barrel pickup, and also jumping. He's very good at all of them.

With Love,
Melinda

SCHOOL DAYS

Consolidation? No Thanks

In the first half of the 1900s, most Amish kids here went to the public schools. These days, nearly all of them are in Amish parochial schools. So, what happened? In a word, "consolidation."

Before 1950, schools tended to be small, rural, and controlled by the local parents. Some Amish fathers even served on public school boards. But as the small schools were consolidated into large districts beginning in the 1950s, the Amish became more and more hesitant about sending their children off on buses to faraway, centralized schools.

It is a central rule of the Amish culture that formal education ends after eighth grade. This bothers some outsiders, but I'm not going to attempt to either judge or defend that issue here. The bottom line is, the Supreme Court determined in Wisconsin v. Yoder in 1972 that for Amish children, an eighth-grade education was sufficient to equip them for their way of life, and nothing further was required of them in terms of formal education.

So they began buying up the no-longer-needed rural one-room schoolhouses, and they opened their own schools. This kept their children near home and their parents in charge of their education. Amish students normally walk to school, or take a pony cart, or most often, they ride a bicycle. Each church district or two has their own school, with a three-member board to hire the teachers, maintain the property, approve the curriculum, and take care of the finances.

In this area, one Amish school was opened in the 1940s; one in the 1950s; eighteen in the 1960s; six in the 1970s; nine in the 1980s; seventeen in the 1990s; twenty-one from 2000-2010; and fifty-two since 2010.

These days, the supply of abandoned one-room schoolhouses is long gone, so the Amish build their own buildings, such as the one pictured here.

A few Amish children in our area still attend public schools, mixed in with English children, but that is getting more rare as the years go by.

One Room Schools Are Alive and Well

So, what are Amish schools like?

An Amish child begins first grade at age seven. Up until this time they have spoken only "Dutch" at home (a colloquial form of German unique to the Amish culture). So the first order of business is learning English, which is the language used in their schools. Most of them have picked up some English by this time by paying attention to the adults and older kids, but they haven't spoken it.

Most have one room, divided in half with a curtain, and staffed by two teachers and possibly a teacher's assistant. One teacher might have grades 1-2 and 5-6, and the other might have grades 3-4 and 7-8. That way, the older ones can help the younger ones. But they can also be divided according to how many students are in each grade. A few have a third classroom for "special education" students or for some other reason. There are generally about 35-40 students; any more than that, and the school district is split in two.

Most schools have playground equipment, a ball diamond or two, and perhaps a basketball hoop, and the children can be seen playing softball at recess. There are also bike racks, a hitching post, and usually a small outbuilding for storage. I've read things about Amish schools having outhouses, but that's not true, at least not around here! There are indoor restrooms, one for boys and one for girls. Many have a downstairs area for storage and/or social events. Newer schools have living quarters for two teachers. Many have an old-fashioned bell on top, with a rope which the teacher can pull to call the children in.

The subjects taught are set down in a booklet called "Regulations and Guidelines for Amish Parochial Schools of Indiana," published by the Amish leaders to help their local school boards follow the state guidelines. The curriculum minimums include:

- Reading (including phonics for younger students) – at least 4 times weekly
- Math (including fractions, decimals, and measurements) – at least 4 times weekly
- English (grades 3-8) – at least twice weekly, plus it's the spoken language in school
- Handwriting – at least once a week
- Spelling – at least twice weekly
- Geography and History (one semester of each) – at least twice weekly
- Health and Safety (including buggy safety) – twice weekly for one semester
- Old German (the language of their Bible) – once a week starting in about 3rd grade

Students (or as the Amish say, "scholars") are expected to be well-behaved and respectful. Parents are encouraged to visit the school frequently, and most schools have a guest book for this purpose. Parents are expected to dress their children according to the "ordnung" (rules of the local Amish church); the children's clothes are nearly identical to what their parents wear.

On one of my visits to an Amish school, I was accompanied by a school board member. The teacher had the children stand up, one family group at a time, and the children introduced themselves by name, starting with the oldest in each family. It was very impressive! Other times when I have visited, each child gave his/her name and a quotation or trivia fact they liked, or the children sang a song.

Amish schools must be in session for 167 days per year, which is the Indiana state standard, and school days must be at least five hours long. Their agreement with the State of Indiana requires a 97% daily attendance average, which they usually exceed. Absences for medical appointments, illness, or "attending places where the Word of God is preached" are allowed, but absences for home chores, farm sales, or vacations are not.

The Amish school system's stated goals are to prepare the child for a life of Christian service; the Amish way of life; and the responsibilities of adulthood. From what I've seen, they succeed in those goals quite well.

More Things I've Learned
About Amish Schools

I have a booklet which I borrowed from an Amish school board member that gave lots of information about the Amish school system, so I'll borrow from that booklet here.

There are around 125 Amish schools in the tri-county area (Elkhart, Lagrange, and Noble counties, in northeastern Indiana) as I write this in 2023. Seven new ones were built in 2022! The schools have descriptive names such as Anderson Trail, Scenic Hills, Power Line, Orchard View, Clover Leaf, Hidden Cove, Peaceful Meadow, Cottonwood Grove, Timber Edge, Tollway View, Blue Heron, Little Acorn, and Pigeon River. The newer schools are generally built with white vinyl siding and a shingled or metal roof. Hot water heat is usually built into the floor, and the water well is powered by a battery pack.

Each school is run by a three-man school board consisting of local parents. The schools are grouped into districts of 12-15 schools, and above that, there is a state Amish school board. The tri-county area also has special committees for special education, testing, teacher workshops, and buildings. There is a special new "Schools for Schools" board which endeavors to help with the financing of new schools; counting land costs, a new school can cost $325,000 to build!

Who are the teachers in these schools? They are chosen from within the Amish community itself. The teachers (most are female but not all) will have just an eighth grade education themselves, but they need to have scored at the 10th grade level on the Iowa Test of Basic Skills. The teachers get further training through periodic teachers' meetings (every six weeks) and by reading the Amish teachers' magazine called *The Blackboard Bulletin*. Their pay comes from tuition fees paid by the students, which can run over $2,000 per year per student.

If you wander through Amish Indiana for very long, you'll see one of these buildings, with their yard full of bicycles, their baseball diamonds, and a bell on top, every few miles. It's okay to slow down and get a better look, or even take a few quick photos—as long the children aren't outside playing.

Celebrating Christmas the Amish Way

Last December my husband and I had the privilege of attending two school Christmas programs which included some of our "Amish grandkids"—which is to say, the children of some of our Amish friends. I've known both mothers since before they married, and they now have eleven children between them!

Both programs followed the same basic format: The children presented poems, songs, skits, and short plays, both as a large group and by grade levels. Each school had about 40 students (or "scholars," as they're called).

The first program was at a school in Elkhart County, Indiana, and it lasted about 90 minutes. The classroom had been emptied of desks and set up with benches for the program. There was an elevated stage with a curtain at one end of the room. The room was lit by gaslights in the ceiling and windows all around. (The Amish are very good at making use of natural sunlight!)

I was so impressed at how well-rehearsed the students were, and the great amount of material they had memorized so flawlessly! My favorite part was a song which all the students sang (in German) a song which was called "Kommet Alle Zu Dem Stalle"—which translates as "Come All to the Stable." The children sang the song strongly and clearly, and it was like hearing a choir of angels.

The second program was at a school in St. Joseph County, Michigan, and it lasted about 60 minutes one morning. Both programs had perhaps 150 people in the audience, and we were almost the only English in the crowd both times. The men sat on one side of the room and the women on the other at this program. As always, the front bench on either side was reserved for the small children, so that they could have a good view. The program would be done again in the evening for working parents who couldn't attend during the day, and that one would be "standing room only."

The program consisted of large group songs and also presentations by individual grades and groups. In addition to all the English-language songs, poems, and skits which were performed, the students and the audience at this program sang "Stille Nacht," which is our popular Christmas carol "Silent Night" in German.

After this program there was lots of good food served potluck-style in the school's lower level, and during that time I was able to take a picture of the front half of the schoolroom. I was glad to be able to share this part of Amish life, and it really made it feel like Christmas!

A Brand New Amish Schoolhouse

In early September a few years back, I found myself in a new Amish schoolhouse in the area. I had an hour to kill while my Amish friend talked to the builders about a water system, so I wandered around and took some photos. It was a rare opportunity to be in a brand-new schoolhouse—one of over 125 Amish schoolhouses which can be seen in the Lagrange-Elkhart-Noble county area.

Inside, I found a wall display of the children's names: Louann, Christian, Julia, Kaylene, Lyndon, Sarah, Freeman, Myron, Isaac, Regina, Rachel, Lorraine, Lyle, Martha, Kathryn, Joanna, Jason, Harvey, Orva, Lora, Sharon, Leana, Maryanne, and Linda. That's a good sampling of the typical first names of the next generation of Amish kids. Since last names are so few—20% of the local population are named "Miller" and probably nearly as many are named "Bontrager" or "Yoder"—parents sometimes get creative with the first names.

The empty classroom area had a double set of alphabet posters (in upper case, lower case, and old German script). That's because most schoolhouses have two teachers, and the classroom is divided down the middle by a curtain on a wire. Light is provided by piped-in gas, as well as the large number of windows down each side. Battery-powered lanterns with LED lights are also popular.

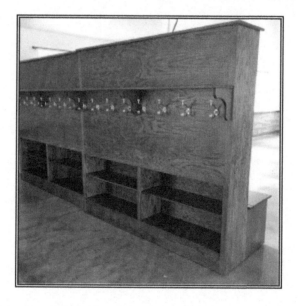

Four of these beautiful oak units separated the open area in the back from the classroom area in the front. The back side had hooks and shelves for the children's coats and things, and the front side had shelving and cabinets for books and school supplies, as well as serving as benches. The units were on casters, so they could be moved aside for school programs and other special events. There was an open area and a pair of restrooms behind the classroom area.

Many newer Amish schoolhouses have living quarters for the teachers. This one was no exception, with a spacious galley kitchen in the back which led to a living room, two bedrooms with closets, and a full bath. The kitchen could also be used for refreshments during school programs and other events.

Something I didn't expect was a copier! I asked my friend where the power came from, and he said it was collected from solar panels on the roof. I'd not seen one of these in an Amish school before, but I've seen them since.

Outside was a baseball field with a very nice backstop, various playground equipment, a long hitching post, and a horse barn.

Several new Amish schoolhouses are built in this area every year, many using this same layout, so this was a good example of what the newest schools look like.

Graduation Time

I had the privilege of being invited to an Amish eighth grade graduation recently. Since formal education ends at the eighth grade, this is a really big deal in the Amish culture.

The graduates are (by law) within three months of their fifteenth birthday when they finish school. The next year or two is spent mostly at home for the girls, sometimes working as a "mother's helper" for women nearby who have recently had a baby—or actually working alongside (and learning things from) their own mothers. The boys typically work on the home farm, or help out an uncle or neighbor.

My friend Queenie and I arrived in the only car to be seen (as I expected). I had a little time to wander, so I looked over the perfect attendance certificates posted on the board, along with essays written by the older kids about their recent field trip to visit other schools in the area.

Each teacher's desk was loaded with simple gifts from the students. The school board also traditionally purchases a gift for each teacher— usually something worth a couple hundred dollars. This year, the gift was a really nice poly outdoor chair that rocked and swiveled.

The ceremony itself consisted of songs and poems and recitations by each of the eight grades, followed by the four graduates (all girls in this case) taking the stage with their diplomas and red roses and performing for the last time as "scholars."

Afterwards there was a potluck meal to die for, which was followed by the traditional students vs. parents baseball game. This game is taken very seriously, and both teams were outside doing pitching, fielding, and batting practice after they finished eating. I didn't stay for the whole game, so I don't know who won this one, but typically they can go either way. I did snap one rather blurry stealth photo before I left.

It was a wonderful day for the girls, as they transition from what, in their culture, is essentially childhood to adulthood. They were proud and excited, and so were their families. I'm glad I could be a part of it.

VISITORS

Be Nice and Play Together!

I have a niece I'll call "Bee." She's grown up now, but when she was young, she used to go to Amish Indiana with me every May, during Mayfest weekend. She enjoyed the food, the shops, the Saturday morning parade, and staying at a bed & breakfast. One thing she wasn't so sure about was meeting my Amish friends.

One year when Bee was about six, we made our May trip. During the usual visit with my Amish friends, Rebecca and I decided that Bee looked bored, just sitting with the grownups and listening to them talk. Rebecca called over her two youngest sons, who were about Bee's age. They were even less sure about Bee than she was about them... Bee was shy, but they were even more so! But I worked on Bee in English, while Rebecca worked on her two boys in "Dutch." I would imagine we were saying the same thing—"Be nice and play together!" All three of the kids looked like they would rather not, but in the end, reluctantly, off the three of them went towards the barn.

Rebecca and I sat down to continue our conversation. A few minutes later we saw the pony cart fly by, with three happy kids in it—one English girl and two Amish boys. They looked like they were having the time of their lives! At one point they got up so much speed that they veered off course, broke through the rock border of Rebecca's vegetable garden, left cart tracks curving through it, and then broke out the other side, rocks flying everywhere! Later, they played with the animals, swung from the rope swing in the hay barn, and then headed for the special swing set featuring a hollow log with a ladder running up through the middle of it. Bee told me later that at one point, they got so used to each other that one of the boys turned to her and asked her something in Dutch.

Bee decided that day that the pony cart was her very favorite thing in Indiana, and she had many more pony cart rides in the years that followed. And I was happy that my cross-cultural friendship with the Amish had been passed down to the next generation.

A Long Way From Estonia

Years ago, before I was married, I used to have European college students stay at my home in suburban Chicago during the summer. Several times over the years, I took some of them to Amish Indiana. I wanted them to see a little more of the great diversity that makes up America.

The first time it was Oliver and Ivan, two young men from Estonia. Four of us traveled the 150 miles east to Shipshewana—the two boys along with my friend Queenie and me. We stayed at Green Meadow Ranch, a bed & breakfast at the north end of Shipshewana.

Both young men loved it there from the first moment. Ivan said to me, "I feel like I breathe differently here—I breathe deeper." I was amazed, because I had often thought the same thing.

After some sightseeing and lots of good food, we ended up at the farm of my oldest and original Amish friends. It was September, and Gerald was harvesting the corn. The green cornstalks had to be cut down at ground level, loaded on wagons, and brought to the chopper that turned the entire plant into "silage"—food for the cattle over the winter. Gerald put us to work right away.

The first few rows around the edge of the cornfield needed to be cut down by hand. Gerald, Queenie, Oliver, and Ivan tossed the corn onto the flat wagon. My job was to drive the two-horse team of Belgian draft horses forward about ten feet, then stop them while corn was tossed onto the wagon, then forward again.

Let me say here, I did not grow up on a farm or around animals—but I did my best. As I drove forward, I alternately ran into the corn, the fence, the corn, and the fence. At one point the two Belgian work horses looked back at me with an unmistakable look that said, "What is wrong with you?" I didn't know that horses can give you the stink eye!

But eventually we got the wagon loaded and Gerald drove it to the silage chopper, where we threw the stalks onto the conveyor belt, being careful to keep our hands clear of the chopper!

Although tractors are not allowed on Amish farms for field work (at this point), they can be used for power. The conveyor belt and silage chopper were run with an old tractor engine which was connected to the chopper by belts. The cornstalks became silage, and then we were done.

It felt good to be more than just a guest, a tourist, or a visitor. And it was a great experience for my young Estonian friends, who were city boys back home. Afterwards, as we enjoyed refreshments in the farmhouse, Gerald produced an atlas and the boys showed him where to find Estonia. Work was done, friendships were formed, and it was an excellent tri-cultural experience for all.

The Lads Meet the Amish
and Almost Crash a Buggy

I wrote in the last chapter about harvesting the corn with two of my foreign-student summer guests, Oliver and Ivan. Another summer, I brought Carl and Anthony to Amish Indiana.

Carl and Anthony ("The Lads" as we called them) were college students from England who had spent the summer in my home. Before they went back home, five of us headed to Amish Indiana— Carl, Anthony, my sister Nancy, my young niece Bee, and me. As usual, I ended up at the farm of my oldest Amish friends. And as usual, they welcomed my guests with hospitality and the same spirit of curiosity about life in England as The Lads had about the Amish way of life.

The Lads got to see a number of farm animals. They were both from English cities—Carl from London and Anthony from Bristol—so the farm culture was a new experience for them. I don't remember if we had homemade baked goods, but I would guess that we did. Then we all went for a buggy ride. Carl sat up front with my Amish friend Gerald, with Bee in the middle, and Anthony and Nancy got into the back seat with me. As it turned out, it was a buggy ride like no other I've had.

At some point Gerald asked Carl if he would like to drive the buggy. Carl happily took the reins, and down the country road we went. At first everything was fine. But at some point we veered off the road and barreled full speed across the front yard of an Amish farm, where two young boys were playing closer to the house. As we sped past them through the middle of their lawn, the boys looked up in surprise—but before they could do anything but stare, we reached the other side of their front yard, crossed the driveway, and veered back onto the road!

What amazed me the most was how calm my Amish friend Gerald was. While I was having a silent nervous breakdown in the back seat, he calmly but swiftly helped Carl get the horses back on the road, as composed as if this happened every day! And down the road we went, Carl saying something British like "Oops, sorry about that."

All in all, a day to remember.

Rick's Bucket List

Do you have a "Bucket List"? My former boss, a lawyer, did. And one of the things on it had to do with his love of horses. Rick has been drawn into my love of Amish Indiana over the years. It started when he met six of my Amish friends when he brought them from Indiana to Illinois for my wedding and they stayed overnight at his home. One day some years later he said to me, "I've always dreamed of driving a six-horse team of Belgian workhorses… Do you think you could make that happen?"

So my Amish friend Gerald and I talked about it… A few conversations later, a plan was in place. The following spring, some time between the beginning of spring field preparation in April and my Amish friends' daughter's wedding in mid-June, my boss and his wife and I would drive to Indiana for three days of fun on the farm.

The time finally arrived, in May of 2012. We arrived at the farm on a Monday afternoon—four of us—my boss, his wife Rose, their visiting friend Olivia, and me. Rick immediately headed off to the fields with Gerald, where he spent most of the next three days doing farm work. Rose and Olivia helped Gerald's wife around the house and visited the local Amish-Mennonite history center. I—who am domestically challenged—spent my time driving one of their daughters around, getting things lined up for her upcoming wedding. I had known this daughter since she was eleven years old, so it was a pleasure to spend so much time talking to her and helping her get things done. We visited the florist, the glass engraver, and lots of other places.

Meanwhile, my boss was having the time of his life. I took this picture of him one afternoon.

On the second afternoon of our visit, I was out and about doing wedding errands when I got a text from Rick. It was a desperate plea: "Please—bring Diet Coke!" So I picked up a few bottles on the way back to the farm, and after arriving, one of the girls said, "I'll ride my horse out and bring it to him." Rick told me later that it was quite a surreal moment, to pause from his farm work to see a young Amish woman riding a horse across the fields to bring him a bottle of Diet Coke!

It was a wonderful three days for us all, and I'm glad I was able to help a friend cross an item off his Bucket List.

Olivia: Costa Rica Meets Amish Indiana

So in 2012 I brought my boss and his wife from Illinois to Amish Indiana, to help him cross something off his bucket list. Accompanying us for this three-day trip was Olivia.

Olivia was not the typical visitor to Amish country. She had lived her whole life in Costa Rica, where she is a language teacher—that's how my boss and his wife had met her. She had been one of their teachers and friends during the year they spent in Costa Rica some time ago, and ever since, she has come to Illinois to visit them on a regular basis. Our trip to Amish Country coincided with her month-long visit to Illinois, so we brought her along.

This photo shows a smiling Olivia getting ready for a ride in the buggy. She thoroughly enjoyed every aspect of the three-day trip—the animals, the food, staying in an Amish home (she had her own room there), riding in the buggy, meeting the children, helping in the kitchen, shopping at the local stores, and visiting Menno-Hof, the local Amish-Mennonite cultural center. At Menno-Hof they brought in a special guide—a former missionary to Latin America—to give her a tour of the center in Spanish.

Olivia's English was what I would call "very spotty." But she did her best to communicate with my Amish friends, with my boss sometimes interpreting for her in a Spanish-English-Pennsylvania Dutch-language triangle. We muddled through, though, and Olivia made herself quite useful around the house while we were there, and even taught the Amish some Spanish phrases. She developed a particularly close bond with one of the daughters of the house who was in her early twenties.

The last day we were there, this same daughter brought out a gift for Olivia. Inside a large plastic ice cream container was a white Amish prayer cap, the type that Amish girls and women wear every day, which she had made by hand. (The ice cream container was to protect the fragile cap on the plane ride back to Costa Rica.) This gift brought tears to Olivia's eyes—or, truth be told, to more eyes than just hers! It was a fitting end to Olivia's Amish experience.

Frank Milks the Cows

My sister Nancy's husband is a native Californian named Frank. They live in suburban Los Angeles, where Frank works in the dairy industry as a vendor of cleaning products and trainer of dairy workers. But he loves to visit Amish Indiana when he and my sister come to the Midwest.

From the very first time he met my Amish friends, they hit it off. We spent the afternoon visiting and talking and eating, and Frank had plenty to talk about, since he works in the dairy industry and they are dairy farmers. Soon it was 4 p.m.—milking time—and my Amish friend Gerald asked Frank if he wanted to come out and watch the milking. Frank replied, "No—I want to help with the milking." Gerald said, "Are you sure? You'll get really dirty!" but Frank said, "That's okay with me."

So out they went… Nancy and I watched from behind the red gates you can see in this picture of the milking barn, as Frank put on tall muck boots and went to work. The first group of eight cows were brought into the barn and put in their places. Frank's job was to clean the udders and attach the milking machine to each animal. Health regulations require the use of milking machines; the Amish farmers power them with diesel generators set up out behind their barns.

They also use the generators to power the big metal cooling tanks where the milk is kept.

Frank worked his way from animal to animal, working alongside Gerald and his sons. The second group of cows was brought in, and then the third. Frank was having the time of his life.

Soon the work was done, and the men took showers in the special washroom at the back of the farmhouse. Frank was all smiles, and he understood in a new way where the milk came from that was processed in the plants around Los Angeles where he worked every day.

Since then Frank has been back to visit my friends, and the next time he was able to give them some helpful advice on how to get the already-low bacteria count in their milk even lower. (The lower the count, the higher the price they get for the milk.) And I am always glad for yet another connection between my Amish friends and my own "English" family.

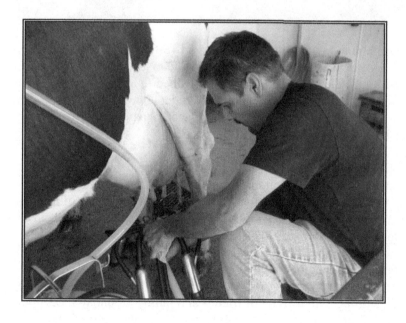

Lorin's Amish Adventure

Even though my family is from the Midwest, my sister has lived in the Los Angeles area for many years. She married a wonderful California native named Frank, and I gained four nieces and nephews in the bargain. One of them is Lorin, and a few years back while I still lived in suburban Chicago, Lorin accompanied my sister, her husband Frank, and me to Amish Indiana.

Lorin, in her late teens at the time, is a California girl through and through, but she loves animals, so we thought we might be able to entertain her there for a couple of days. We stayed at one of my favorite B&Bs (Hidden Creek), visited some local shops, and had a homemade pretzel at JoJo's—a local specialty. We decided that the best place to find animals was at an Amish farm, so off we went one afternoon to hang out with my Amish friends.

I have brought all manner of friends and family around to meet my Amish friends, and they invariably greet my newest arrivals with hospitality (and some measure of amusement, I think). After touring the farm and meeting farm animals of every size and description, we piled into the buggy for a ride.

An Amish buggy is a great way to see the countryside. Lorin sat in front with my Amish friend, and the rest of us squeezed in the back, and off we went. It wasn't long before Lorin was driving the buggy. From my seat in the back I was able to take photos unseen, and I got this second one during our ride. Lorin took to driving a buggy like a native.

Today I emailed Lorin and asked her what she remembered most about the trip. She mentioned the pretzels, and the fact that the young Amish kids she met didn't speak English. And of course she remembered the various animals, and watching the cows be milked, and the little pony cart she rode around in at another Amish farm we visited.

Lorin took to the entire experience as few other California teenagers could have done. She's a fan of my writing now, and a fan of Amish Indiana, too—and I'm glad.

GARY AND ME

Friendship and Knee Surgery

I still remember the trip to Amish Indiana years ago when my new husband finally became comfortable around the Amish. It was the time that Gerald had knee surgery.

Gerald had torn up his knee sliding into third base during a family game of baseball the previous summer. (I guess men are just overgrown boys in any culture!) One December when we were out visiting, Gerald told us that the doctor had said that surgery was needed, and he was obviously feeling out of his comfort zone as he talked about it. My husband, after conferring with me for agreement, said, "We can come out here and take you there—would that help?"

So plans were made… We would come out from Illinois on a Thursday night, spend the night at the farm (something my husband had said he'd never do), and then on Friday we would take Gerald and Rebecca to the surgery center fifteen miles away, sit with her while he was in surgery, and then drive them to the pharmacy and home.

The time came, and out we went. Late that Thursday evening we settled in with Gerald, Rebecca, and their 14-year-old son to play a few games of dominoes by gaslight. It was a game my husband and I had to be taught—another step back to a simpler time! Things were going along just fine until there was a ruckus outside. A steer had broken out of his pen at the Angus beef farm down the road, and he was running renegade through the snow in the dark, breaking through any fences that got in his way. The men (except for my husband) dropped everything and ran out to assist, and that was the end of dominoes!... Later that night we slept under a homemade quilt, with an electric lantern by the bed.

The next morning we headed to the surgery center, and I do think that having us along made a difference. We knew where to go and what to do and what to expect, and Rebecca didn't have to wait by herself. Gerald's surgery went well, and we were able to get him his prescriptions on the way home. So it all worked out... and after that, my husband was as comfortable around the Amish as I could hope for. Now he felt like they were his friends, too.

My Amish Friends Come to Chicagoland

In 2007, one day not long after I got engaged, my boss asked me, "Have you thought about having your Amish friends at your wedding?" My answer was, "I've thought about it every day." I'd brought my fiancée out to meet them, and they liked him and were thrilled that I was finally "settling down." But I didn't think there was a way to have them attend the wedding—after all, they lived 150 miles away, and the logistics would be more than I could handle that weekend.

My boss had been thinking about it, too, or he wouldn't have asked the question—and he had a plan. He offered to rent a 7-passenger van; drive over that Friday; bring back six of my friends; have them stay at his house Friday night; bring them to the wedding on Saturday; and then drive them home on Saturday evening, in time for them to attend church at home on Sunday morning. I was overjoyed.

The next task: Deciding which six to invite. I quickly decided on Gerald and Rebecca, my two original Amish friends, and two of their daughters with spouses—the oldest two—the two who had invited me to their weddings several years earlier. In the end, one of the daughters was just too nervous to come, but her younger brother and his wife came in their place. Gerald said to me, "Well, Sue, we're nervous. But we're coming."

How to make them less nervous, I thought to myself?... So I printed out three copies of the entire wedding script and mailed them out. I also assured them that there would be no alcohol, no loud music, and no dancing at the reception—just food, quiet music, and socializing.

The time came, and they arrived. I decided they might be more relaxed if they met the wedding party and families the night before, so I invited them to the rehearsal dinner at our new home. They arrived looking very nervous indeed! But half an hour later they were eating and talking and having a fine time. The next day, after asking the wedding photographer to not take any pictures of them, they settled in at the church, and I still remember the beaming smile I got from Rebecca as I walked back down the aisle at the end of the ceremony.

It was so special to share my big day with my friends from a different culture who had been so accepting of a middle-aged, unmarried woman in their midst all those years. After being invited to two of their weddings, it was wonderful to return the favor!

Why Not Start Our Retirement With a Bang?

So, maybe it's time I explained a few things…

Sometimes people who visit my Facebook page or website think that I've always lived in Amish Indiana—but that's not the case. We moved here in 2017. Before that, though, it was my favorite place for weekend getaways for decades!

So, in a 2016, we got serious about retiring and moving from Illinois to Indiana. We decided to retire on July 1, 2017.

By November 2016 we had purchased a ranch house in Middlebury, Indiana and—unexpectedly quickly—sold our home in Yorkville, Illinois. It was time to move our clothes and few pieces of furniture to a rented condo in Yorkville, and everything else to Middlebury! My husband spent lots of weekends moving trailer-loads of our stuff east on the tollway, and I spent my weekends unpacking it and making it seem like home. But it had to be just a weekend place for the time being. Patience!

As 2017 rolled in, our plans quickly changed because of two very unexpected "acts of God"—first late in the winter, Gary's place of employment (Pilkington in Naplate, Illinois) was blown apart by a tornado—and then in early spring, I found out I had stage 3 thyroid cancer.

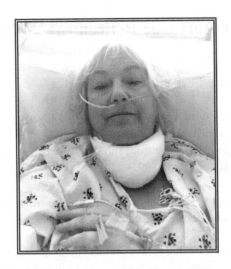

It was time to accelerate our plan! Thank goodness we had moved ninety percent of our things over to Indiana the previous fall, because although I had done my cancer surgery in Illinois, I still had radiation therapy ahead of me in Indiana and I was weak as a kitten. By late May I was living in Middlebury, my loyal and faithful sister Nancy at my bedside, and Gary followed in early June.

After I was declared cancer-free in July, I thought, "Why not really make this year even more special?" So I had a knee replacement in October and another one in December.

So, that's how it happened... After a pretty brutal first year here, I feel blessed to be alive and healthy and living in Amish Indiana with my soul mate. Sometimes dreams do come true.

Who Knew?! A City Girl Learns a Few Things

I moved to Amish Indiana from suburban Chicago, after retiring from seventeen years as an administrative assistant at a law firm, and before that, nineteen years of classroom teaching. One thing I've learned since I moved here is this: My childhood on Grandpa and Grandma Erickson's farm, and 30 years of being a tourist over here, didn't teach me everything there was to know about country life!

Here are eight City Girl things I believed until embarrassingly recently. Feel free to laugh at me—I can't hear you! Or, feel free to learn something, if you're a City Slicker too.

1. **There are two types of corn.** Most corn is "field corn," which is used for silage (animal feed—the entire plant while still green), or

seed corn, or ethanol production, or it's ground up for corn meal. But some corn is "sweet corn," and that's the kind that becomes corn on the cob. Don't try to boil up field corn and eat it with butter!

2. **Corn stalks usually have only one ear of corn per stalk.** That is not how we drew corn when I was in elementary school! There was always an ear on the left, then the right, and then the left again. But no—one ear of corn per stalk is the norm. A couple of my Amish friends had a good laugh over this one... Apparently, if corn is spaced out when it's planted, a plant may send up a second stalk with a second ear of corn. But these days, the Amish plant their rows 30 inches apart with between 28,000 and 32,000 kernels (seeds) per acre—wow! And commercial English farms often plant them twice that densely!

3. **Hay is not the same thing as straw.** I'm really embarrassed about this one. But if I can give my Amish friends a laugh, then it's not all bad! "Hay" is one of a number of plants, often alfalfa here, that are harvested while still green and baled up for animals to eat. "Straw" is typically leftover dried-out yellow wheat or oak stalks after the grain is harvested, and it is used for animal "bedding"—under their feet in the stalls to keep things absorbed and cleaner. So, you might say hay vs. straw is like the difference between food vs. toilet paper!

4. **Commercial laying hens don't live long enough to retire and move in with their kids.** There are dozens of free-range egg houses around here these days. Each egg barn can hold as many as 20,000 laying hens, as this one does—these long, narrow buildings are huge! My friend Galen told me that the hens (his are Lohman Browns) start laying at about 4 months old, quickly working up to about one egg a day. At about 21 months old their egg production tapers off sharply, and so after an egg-laying career of less than two years, it's off to the meat packing plant to be "repurposed," sometimes for stewing meat but usually for pet food. Backyard hen enthusiasts can keep their laying hens for many years, in spite of lower egg production, but for commercial egg producers, it's not economically feasible to do so.

5. **Not all sheep are the same.** I talked about this in another chapter... Some sheep are bred to have wool, and others, called "hair sheep," are bred for their meat (lamb or mutton). They're

not the same. You can't get good wool from a hair sheep, nor good meat from a wool sheep.

6. **Stallions are rare, geldings are not.** I always thought horses came in two varieties, mares and stallions. But it turns out that, in this horse-and-buggy culture where virtually everyone owns at least a few horses, stallions are rare and the vast majority are gelded (neutered). I asked an Amish friend of mine with a lot of horse expertise about this, and he said that for buggy horses, work horses, and ponies alike, the rate of neutering is about 90%. He said that stallions are "unruly in the barn" and the only reason to have one is for stud purposes. The same holds true for cattle— very few males are kept as bulls for breeding—bulls are far too dangerous to keep around unless absolutely necessary. A couple of years ago, a local Amish farm wife was killed by their bull for no worse offense than just being in his pasture when he was in a bad mood.

7. **Horses get hit by lightning.** Both buggy horses and draft horses have the habit of heading for the biggest tree when a thunderstorm hits, to try to stay dry. Consequently, they sometimes can get hit (and killed) by lightning. My friend Gerald has lost one this way, and he once told me about a friend of his who lost four at one time, when they huddled under a tall tree that was struck.

8. **Being a dairy cow isn't exactly a full time job.** Or rather, it is a two-part job—producing milk and producing calves. A dairy cow (mostly Holsteins around here, or Jerseys) don't give milk 365 days a year. Rather, they "freshen" for about six to eight weeks every year, when they don't give milk at all. Incredibly to me, about six to eight weeks before a cow is due to have a calf, the way they "dry them out" is by simply not milking them for a few days!

So, I hope you learned something today--and I hope I keep learning!

In Over My Head: My Amish Greenhouse

I got a call a few weeks ago. My husband was doing some plant-hauling for my favorite local greenhouse, Miller's Greenery in Middlebury. The owner wanted to know—was I free on Saturday morning? The family needed to attend their daughter's eighth grade graduation. Could I run the greenhouse for a couple of hours?

I've never worked retail a day in my life—so my first thought was, "What an insane idea!" But that was followed by, "If they think I can do it, maybe I can." And then, "I wonder how many plants I could buy with what they would pay me?"

So, Saturday morning I showed up, and with a total of ten minutes' training, I was off to the races. I kept this diary…

7:00 a.m. – I just woke up to see that my prayers for rain went unanswered. Rats...

9:15 a.m. – Arrival time. I munched on a couple of chewable Alka-Seltzers on the way over to calm my tummy. Mrs. Miller wished me luck and off she went. No customers in sight, which is good, because I'm not sure I can pull this off!

9:30 a.m. – Still alone here. I took some photos just now… Didn't want to do that with customers around, since the Amish don't take kindly to having their pictures taken.

10:10 a.m. – My first sale!—a bottle of Sevin. I'm glad the first one was easy. Another customer is browsing outside.

10:30 a.m. – I just made myself useful! A customer was looking at a "Celebration Maple" but wasn't sure and asked for more information. I whipped out my cell phone, gave him the rundown, and he bought four at $48 each. "Cha-ching!" said the cash register. (Actually, there's no electricity at the greenhouse, so it was a solar calculator and a cash drawer.)

10:55 a.m. – Just did a big sale. So far, customers have come in one at a time with space in between, so I might just make it until noon without driving customers away who got tired of waiting!

11:00 a.m. – Trouble just pulled into the yard in a pickup truck. An English customer says she bought ten ornamental pears last year and paid $40 each instead of the marked price of $48. Can I sell her ten more at the same discount? (Nope.) She walked away empty-handed. I can't authorize that!

11:15 a.m.– A lady wanted to know which watermelon seed variety grows the sweetest fruit. My smartphone to the rescue again!

11:25 a.m. – More customers. A couple more successful sales. Tick, tick, tick…

11:40 a.m. – A woman just bought a 50-pound bag of seed potatoes. Normally the cashier carries purchases out to the customer's buggy and loads them. But I have no upper body strength whatsoever—so I was glad to see that she could heave that bag like it weighed nothing! Amish farm wives are the best!

11:45 a.m. – And here comes the owner's son to take over the store… I'm glad to report that I didn't do any harm (that I know of)—in fact, the owner called to ask me if I'd do it again if they're ever in a pinch! One thing's for sure: I'll be back soon to spend my earnings!

Burnin' Rubber

Okay, some hoodlum "laid a patch" all the way down the road in front of this Amish farm!   Who would do such a thing?? Well… that would be my husband Gary.

It all started when I gave a lift to an Amish acquaintance named Freeman, for whom I'd done a genealogy pedigree chart the previous year. (Amish genealogy is a passion of mine.)

While Freeman and I were driving through the countryside to Nappanee, my phone rang. It was my husband—so there was a roaring engine sound effect and a photo of his street rod on my dashboard display screen.

That got the two of us talking…

You'd be surprised how many of Amishmen had a car or truck when they were young, before putting rumspringa behind them and joining church. Some of them still maintain an interest and a knowledge of all things vehicular. Freeman said how much he'd like to see that car someday, and I told him I'd talk to my husband about bringing it over.

Several months went by, and we didn't get around to following up on it—until a phone message from Freeman reminded us that he hadn't forgotten! So, one evening Gary fired up the hot rod—a reproduction 1932 Ford 3-window coupe that's been turned into to a nostalgia drag racing car.

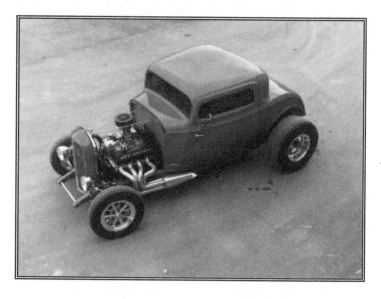

We roared out there and pulled in the driveway, and there was Freeman with five or ten members of his clan, sitting on the front porch or hanging around nearby. This was a big deal to them!

Gary answered some questions and then fired it up. He gave a nice long ride to Freeman first, and we could hear them ripping down a nearby road! That was followed by rides for some of the sons and grandsons. (The girls were nowhere to be seen, other than Freeman's wife, who was content to watch the action from the porch.)

After we were done, we pulled back out onto the road. Gary came to a stop, and I knew what was next—I've been a hot rodder's wife for a sixteen years as of this writing. Gary did a screaming, roaring smoky burnout that turned into what hot rodders call "laying a patch" of rubber in two ribbons down the road.

We happened to drop by a few days later and I took a picture of the two ribbons of burnt rubber on the road. Freeman said after we left, his son paced out the tire marks on the road, and they were 120 feet long! He also said that the cloud of smoke wafted from the road over the pastures and didn't dissipate the rest of the evening. But as he pointed out to Gary, "It did keep the mosquitoes away."

Gary has taken other Amish friends for a ride in his street rod—unlike most drag cars, it has a passenger seat and some safety equipment, and so it's a street-legal car. When cultures collide, it can be a lot of fun!

Talkin' Dutch

As I've mentioned before, the Amish are actually a tri-lingual people.

There's "Pennsylvania Dutch" or "Dutch," the colloquial form of German that is their mother tongue. As time goes on, more and more English words creep into the Dutch, kind of like they've crept in to Spanish to make "Spanglish."

Then there's English. That's the language of their formal education, so they learn to read, write, and speak it when they start school. Then lastly, there's "German." This is an old German, similar to what was spoken in Europe in the 1600s. Old German is the language of the Amish hymnbook and Bible.

So, after six years of living here, I've become very fluent in Pennsylvania Dutch.

No, actually, I've made a very poor start! Here's what I know, and it ain't much:

- "Vie bisht du?" That means, "How are you?"
- "Vo bisht du?" That means, "Where are you?"
- "Hops ga du fa dich." That means, "I did that for you; I took care of that."
- "Esse" means "eat," as in Essenhaus Restaurant.
- "Mom" and "Dad" are the same as Mom and Dad in English.
- "Dawdi" is how they say Grandpa, and Grandma is "Mommy." Thus, farms might have a "Dawdi Haus," which is where the grandparents live. Some of my little Amish friends have called me "Mommy Sue," which melts my heart!
- "Youngies" are the "young people"—those who are sixteen or older. Some have joined the Amish church, and some haven't. "Youngies" might go to singings on Sunday nights, and they have lots of other social activities. There are 2,000-3,000 youngies in this community.
- "Rumspringa" is literally "running around," and it's the name for what the youngies do from their 16th birthday until they join church (as 90% of them do). But I won't open that can of worms today!

So it's safe to say that my Amish friends and I switch to English when conversing! But I do enjoy listening to them speak Dutch and trying to pick out enough words to get the gist of what they're saying.

As I said, English has crept into Pennsylvania Dutch. For instance, the Amish way to say "goodbye" is "see ya."

They also have their own way of speaking English sometimes... Instead of "in the morning," they say "in the forenoon." Someone who has left the Amish has "jumped the fence." And if they want to know if something is okay with you, the Amish say, "if that'll suit."

Also interesting to me are the Amish figures of speech. They have some of the same ones we do, but also some unique ones, and I will give an example here (in English)... Instead of saying someone is "not hitting on all eight cylinders" or "not playing with a full deck," they might say, "He's got a couple of noodles hanging off the plate." I wish I knew more of these! I'm gonna start paying more attention.

WHOOPIE PIES AND OTHER TREATS

Whoopie Pies

Of all the treats that I buy and enjoy in Amish Indiana—and there are plenty—one of my favorites is the "whoopie pie."

"What is a whoopie pie," you ask? According to Wikipedia, it is "a U.S. baked good that may be considered either a cookie, pie, or cake. It is made of two round mound-shaped pieces of chocolate cake, or sometimes pumpkin or gingerbread cake, with a sweet, creamy filling or frosting sandwiched between them." Yeah, that describes it pretty well. My son-in-law, who lives in western Pennsylvania, calls them "gobs."

Wikipedia goes on to say that the origin of the name is uncertain, but they are a New England and Pennsylvania Amish tradition, probably brought over from Germany by the Amish. Women would make them from cake batter leftovers and put them in their husbands' lunch pails. The whoopie pie is the official state treat of Maine (not to be confused with Maine's official state dessert, which is blueberry pie). I'll bet you didn't know that.

As with most food items, the quality varies, and the fresher, the better. The best whoopie pies I've ever had were baked by the teenage daughter of one of my Amish friends. She knew I loved them, so she made them whenever she knew I was coming and sent me home with a plateful. Now she's in her twenties and married with a home of her own. I miss those whoopie pies, so I've had to seek out another source for my addiction. The best ones I've found are made at Essenhaus Bakery in Middlebury, where they have the basic flavors, and also a "whoopie pie flavor of the month." The flavor for this past January was mocha, and they were heavenly.

I see online that there is a bakery in Maine that specializes in whoopie pies called wickedwhoopies.com! They sell them for $26 a dozen plus shipping. They look good, and pretty true to the Amish Indiana tradition, except the filling is a little thicker, and they have some unusual flavors like 'Lip Lick'n Lemon' and Orange. They sell regular-sized whoopies, mini-whoopies, and a jumbo, five-pound whoopie! The founder says she has made over four million whoopie pies in fifteen years, and her product was featured on the Oprah show.

Anyway—should you find yourself in Amish Indiana, why not try something new and different? And if you have a sweet tooth like I do, why not make it a whoopie pie?

Soft Pretzels: Not Like the Bagged Kind

So—once again, my husband has found his way into one of my stories—and as usual, he has food in his hands and a smile on his face. The reason this time is a hand-rolled, fresh-baked, yeasty, buttery, warm, soft pretzel. These are a common treat in both Amish Indiana and Lancaster County, Pennsylvania, and we've been known to grab a beverage and make a meal out of them!

The recipe for soft pretzels is available all over the internet and in Amish cookbooks. The ingredients are simple: flour, sugar, salt, yeast, warm water, egg, butter, and coarse salt for sprinkling on top. When they are bought at a pretzel place, dipping sauces are usually available. The traditional dips are sweet or spicy mustard, but offerings these days include choices such as cheddar cheese, cream cheese, marinara, nacho cheese, vanilla icing, caramel, or hot fudge. (But we like them plain! You can't improve on perfection.)

But where did soft pretzels come from?

The website for the oldest pretzel factory in the United States, JuliusSturgis.com, says that the Palatine Germans—known on our side of the pond as the "Pennsylvania Dutch"—brought pretzels with them when they came to the United States in the 1800s. (Other sites say it was the 1700s.)

I learned on TodayIFoundOut.com that the Sturgis Pretzel Factory was founded in 1861 in Lititz, Pennsylvania. The soft pretzel came first; the hard pretzel came later. The website says, "It's believed that Sturgis' factory was the first to develop hard pretzels. These crunchy, salty snacks lasted longer in an airtight environment than soft pretzels did, allowing them to be sold in stores far away from the bakery and kept on shelves much longer." Even today, 80% of American pretzels are made in Pennsylvania.

One more thing: If you can't just drop everything and head to Amish Indiana or Pennsylvania for a pretzel, here's the next best thing— head to the mall and purchase a pretzel from Auntie Anne's. Quoting from the website amish365.com:

> "Perhaps the most well-known Amish pretzel baker is Anne Beiler, founder of the Auntie Anne's Pretzel chain... She was born into an Amish home in Pennsylvania, but the family switched to the Mennonite faith when she was a child. She started selling pretzels from a farmers market stand years ago and now sits atop a pretzel empire with outlets all over the world."

Amish Peanut Butter—Give It a Try!

I've not been a big fan of peanut butter, at least not as an adult… As a child I was a pretty finicky eater, and I ate way too much of the stuff when whatever was on the table didn't suit me. Since then, I've had no taste for it—or at least, I didn't until my Amish friend Rebecca introduced me to something they make which is commonly known as "Amish peanut butter."

When it's sold in the local stores it's often called "Amish Church Peanut Butter." This is because it is made as part of the standard after-church meal. The Amish don't have church buildings—they hold church on their farms. After the three-hour service, the host family feeds everyone a cold lunch before sending them home.

The meal is pretty standard and unchanging. It makes sense to do it that way… Hosting church is a stressful task. Everything is cleaned and scrubbed as the family tries to put their best foot forward for their guests. Imagine the added stress if the hostess had to try to equal or outdo the previous hostess on the noon meal, continually worrying about "keeping up with the Yoders." It made more sense to standardize the meal. And part of that meal is Amish peanut butter.

How does it differ from what we're used to? I've seen various recipes in Amish cookbooks, but typically it's a blend of peanut butter, marshmallow fluff, and some type of sweetener—perhaps honey or Karo syrup. So it's lighter and sweeter than regular peanut butter and it is oh-so-good! It's sold all over Amish Indiana, but it's not cheap—although it's more reasonably priced at the places the locals shop, like E&S Foods. It's also on the table in many restaurants here.

Some of my Amish friends save me a margarine-tub of Amish peanut butter whenever they make it for church—and sometimes I just get a spoon and eat it out of the tub like ice cream. Lately I've taken to breaking off little pieces of dark chocolate Ghirardelli bars and dipping them. I suppose a person could also eat it on bread or toast, like it's meant to be eaten.

Amish Church Peanut Butter. One more reason I like Amish Indiana.

Don't Boil Maple Syrup in the House

So, it's that time of year (March as I write this)—buckets have appeared on maple trees all over Amish Indiana. It's time to make maple syrup! Ads are appearing in The People's Exchange for maple syrup supplies, and posters can be seen all over town for maple syrup festivals, maple syrup cooking demonstrations, and other ways to celebrate the spring ritual.

I wondered how maple syrup is made, so I looked to TapMyTrees.com. I found out that sugar maples are the best trees to tap, but black, red, or silver maples also work. The sap starts to flow in February or March, and the best weather is alternating warm and cold—it gets the sap flowing. Trees should be 12" in diameter or more, and bigger trees can have multiple taps. The sap typically flows for four to six weeks, and tapping stops when the temperatures remain above freezing and the leaves start to come out.

The basics are simple: Drill a upward-slanting hole 2 to 2.5 inches deep, then hammer in the metal tap and hang a clean bucket from the hook on the tap or connect to the bucket with a tube. Sap starts to flow immediately, and it looks like water. It may drip slowly, or it may fill a bucket in a day or two.

Then it's just a matter of collecting the sap buckets, filtering out the impurities, and then boiling off the excess water, which turns the maple sap into maple syrup. The syrup is done when it's thick and golden. The sap-to-syrup ratio varies, depending on whom you ask— some sources say as little as 10-to-1, but most say much higher. Someone at our church makes a few gallons of maple syrup every year, and he gave us a pint the other day. I asked him how many gallons of sap it takes to make a gallon of syrup, and he said it takes forty! That's why his is so good.

One caution—don't try this in the kitchen! This warning comes from Rink Mann on MotherEarthNews.com:

> The main thing about making maple syrup is you have to boil off about 32 quarts of water in the form of steam to end up with one quart of maple syrup. That means that if you're boiling down a batch some Saturday afternoon on the kitchen stove and are aiming for three quarts of syrup, you're going to put about 24 gallons of water into the air before the boiling's done. Unless you've got one powerful exhaust fan, you'll end up with water streaming down the walls and enough steam to impair visibility across the room. And, when things finally do clear, you're apt to find the wallpaper lying on the floor. Then, too, even if the batch doesn't boil over, which it can, the sugar spray from all that furious boiling gets all over the stove and is harder than blazes to get off. So, if you want to maintain a measure of domestic tranquility, it's best to do your boiling outside, or in a handy garage or shed.

Sound advice for a good marriage *and* good maple syrup.

Selling Walnuts

Did you ever wonder where your grocery-store walnuts come from? They may have come from Amish Indiana.

My Amish friend Lily used to clean a few wealthy people's houses for extra income. At one of them, one of her yearly tasks was to remove the hundreds of fallen walnuts from the lawn. One year she collected them in old feed bags and brought them home.

A few days after this task was completed, Lily phoned me, and we loaded six or seven bags of walnuts into the back of my SUV. Off we went to a nearby Amish farm located between Middlebury and Shipshewana. (Or should I say, she loaded them—I'm a city girl and I have about one-tenth the strength of the average Amish woman!)

The farmer had an ancient Hammons black walnut huller – a big green machine that could crack the tough outer hull but leave the inner shell that we're all familiar with, intact.

So, the gas engine was fired up, and the bags were unloaded into the metal hopper one by one. The walnuts went up a conveyor belt and into the depths of the machine. Down a chute on the left side came the walnuts and into green bags.

Out the other side came the shredded hulls, which went by conveyor belt into an old wooden farm wagon to be spread on the fields. Nothing is wasted!

In the end, Lily sold 200+ pounds of walnuts, so at $15 per 100 pounds, she was written a check for $32. I remarked that it seemed like a lot of work for $32—but as she pointed out, the homeowner she cleaned for had paid her by the hour to pick up the walnuts, so this was just a bonus!

She said that sometimes, on Amish farms with walnut trees, selling walnuts is a nice project for the children of the family—they can all help gather up the walnuts into bags, and then the money can be used for something special and fun.

By the time we were ready to leave, there were two Amish buggies in line behind my SUV. The owner said that last year on the last day of walnut season, there were buggies lined up all the way down the gravel driveway and then down the road—a three-hour wait!

The walnuts are then sent off for further processing along the farm-to-table food chain. So think of that next time you buy a bag of walnuts!

Time to Make the Doughnuts

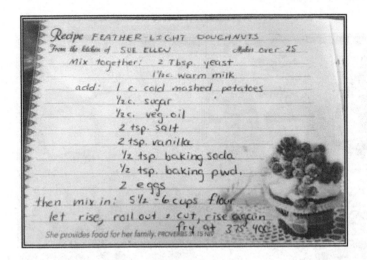

Recipe FEATHER LIGHT DOUGHNUTS
From the kitchen of SUE ELLEN   Makes over 25
Mix together: 2 Tbsp. yeast
                1½ c. warm milk
add: 1 c. cold mashed potatoes
      ½ c. sugar
      ½ c. veg. oil
      2 tsp. salt
      2 tsp. vanilla
      ½ tsp. baking soda
      ½ tsp. baking pwd.
      2 eggs
then mix in: 5½ - 6 cups flour
let rise, roll out & cut, rise again
                     fry at 375°-400°
She provides food for her family. PROVERBS 31:15 NIV

A few weeks ago I found myself at an Amish farm in Michigan on a pleasant Saturday afternoon. Ten of us women and girls (and one baby) had just spent a few hours garage-sale-shopping, while the men went out fishing on a nearby lake. I was the English friend and driver.

Now it was time for the ladies to relax in the big kitchen while the kids played outside and the men kept fishing… Pretty soon lunch had been eaten, and the matriarch of the clan, my friend Rebecca, started making doughnuts—a process I'd never seen before, except at a Krispy Kreme store. Turns out it's not that much different.

The basic ingredients are shown in this recipe, which has the unique twist of adding a cup of cold mashed potatoes! (My friend used mashed potato flakes instead.) A doughnut mix can be used to speed things up, adding sugar, yeast, and warm water.

The dough was left in a bowl to rise while we had our lunch. Then it was rolled out, and circles were cut with an upside-down tumbler. A little heart cutter made the center holes, and some of the leftover pieces (what my mother-in-law would call "snibbles") were saved, too. The dough was given time to rise again.

Then a few at a time, she dropped them into a pan of hot oil, flipped them over after a minute or two, and laid them on paper towels. Five or six dozen doughnuts went in and out of the oil (plus the holes and snibbles).

In the meantime, one of Rebecca's daughters had been mixing up powdered sugar and water for the glaze. Now she dipped them one or two at a time, letting the glaze drip off from a long fork (a trick she learned from her mother). Not all of them made it into the glaze—I periodically swiped one from the assembly line!

Now another daughter sprang into action, packing the cooled doughnuts into Tupperware containers (with four for me to take home to my doughnut-loving husband). They were hot, fresh, and delicious. And many hands made light work!

LIFE AND DEATH

Singing to Mrs. R.

In autumn of 2017 I was visiting this Amish farm with Gary, who was discussing having a pole barn built for us with Steve, an Amish carpenter. Meanwhile, his wife Martha and I and my friend Rebecca were chatting at the kitchen table—the usual thing.

Before long, an elderly Amish lady hobbled in (she had a bad knee) and joined us; she was Steve's mother, and she lived in the dawdi haus (grandparent house) adjoining the main house.

Something about her just struck me. Maybe it was her sweet voice and demeanor; maybe it was the fact that she reminded me of my late grandmother; maybe it was just my little voice telling me to pay attention. She was a widow—her husband had died many years ago, leaving her with twelve children (nine still at home). All were now grown, and most had joined the Amish church.

I went home that day and couldn't get her out of my mind. In fact, I was awake most of the night, to my husband's bewilderment. I felt like I should play some part in her life—but I couldn't figure out what it was. She was well taken care of by her son and her extended family, and wasn't "needy" in any way.

A few weeks later, she took a turn for the worse. Her bad knee failed her completely, and during the course of dealing with that, she had a stroke.

I went to see her, and Mrs. R. was much changed. Her family said sadly that she wasn't even responsive most of the time—but we sat down anyway, if only to chat with the family. When Mrs. R. realized I was there, she perked up and lifted her head, her eyes lit up, and a big smile came over her face. For some strange reason, my presence cheered her up!

So I began to visit her regularly. But what could I offer? She had plenty of company—I could see that from her guest book.

After my second or third visit, I was singing a hymn as I drove home, and it hit me: I could sing to her! The Amish church hymns are long and complex and sung in German, but the Amish also sing many of our familiar English hymns, which they learn in their youthful "Sunday night singing" days.

Sure enough, Mrs. R. loved being sung to. Her daughter-in-law told me that she had always loved music, and it was hard for her being housebound in recent times and missing church. As I sang hymn after hymn, her face would light up.

150

It's the dead of winter in 2018 as I write this, and I'm still visiting Mrs. R. every week if I can, and I'm still bringing my hymnbook. She's getting better now and she can talk a little, although it's a struggle to do so—and she is building up her strength. I don't know how this story will end. I only know that she has been more of a blessing to me than I can say.

* * * * * * * * * * *

A few weeks ago I was thinking about driving over to sing for Mrs. R. I try to stop about once a week. I left a message with her daughter-in-law Martha, asking if Thursday was okay. She said, "I'm taking Mom to her elderly aunt's house on Thursday. Her sister and some nieces will be there, too. Why don't you come over there and join us?"

So the next morning I found myself driving to the address she gave me, near Shipshewana, with my hymnal on the passenger seat. My destination was a snug little dawdi haus on an Amish farm, home of Mrs. R.'s 92-year-old aunt.

I walked in to find a busy dining room with a long table full of food. Around it were eleven Amish women, ages 35 to 92, eating and talking. A few of their small children played on the floor in the living room. When I walked in, the room went silent and all of them looked up at me. My friend Martha quickly said, "We saved you a spot over here, at the head of the table!" Yikes! I'm not usually nervous in any Amish situation, but this was throwing me a little. But I made my way to the far end of the table. The others had been eating for half an hour already, so they said, "Why don't you have something to eat, and we'll sing to you!"

So I sat and ate while these eleven wonderful Amish ladies sang to me… Then I sang to them… Then we sang together.

By the time I left, I had made some new acquaintances, and one of the ladies took me aside and said, " I know my mother would really like it if you came over and sang to her some time." I promised that I would get her name and address from my friend, and I will.

* * * * * * * * * * *

Earlier today, I drove over to sing to Mrs. R. again. This time, her widowed sister was here from Arkansas for a visit. She's a sweet older lady whom I've met before. After we realized we both like genealogy and talked about that for a while, I got out my hymnbook to sing.

Around the middle of my second song, Mrs. R.'s sister disappeared— and reappeared with a harmonica. By the start of my third song, we had figured out how to start out on the same key.

So we serenaded Mrs. R. together for a little while on a dark autumn day, under an electric lantern in a cozy Amish farmhouse. I've never sung with a harmonica before, but it was otherworldly and wonderful. And most importantly, Mrs. R. enjoyed it.

Saying Goodbye to Mrs. R.

It's September 2021, and yesterday I said goodbye to my beloved Mrs. R.

In the last few months, an ulcerated leg, which she was able to recover from last year, flared up on the other leg—and this time, nothing could be done, and hospice was called in. Her body was just too tired to win this battle—and so a few weeks ago, I knew that my days with her were numbered. I visited her about two weeks before she died, when she could no longer sit in her wheelchair. As I sang to her, she sometimes opened her eyes—and always smiled at me, as she had so many times before.

I first met Mrs. R. four years ago. Martha, her main caregiver and daughter-in-law, would make me some coffee, and sometimes Steve and Martha and I would sit around their kitchen table and talk. But mostly I came to sing…

Although her stroke had left her unable to talk much, Mrs. R. would smile and smile at me as I sang, and her sterling silver blue eyes would sparkle. Sometimes she would be able to sing along with me—"Some glad morning, when this life is over, I'll fly away…"

We always ended with "Jesus Loves Me," and any family members who happened to be in the house would join in and sing it with us.

Martha (and the other family members who sometimes took turns caring for Mrs. R. in their homes) thanked me regularly for coming over and told me how much my visits meant to their mother. But it was I who was being blessed! The more I sang to Mrs. R., the more I loved her—and the more time I spent with her, the more she became like the sweet elderly mother I never really had.

A few days before she died, I came to sing once more. By this time, she had become mostly unresponsive, but I sang anyway… Several times she opened her eyes and I saw the old smile. As always, I ended with "Jesus Loves Me"—and her eyes opened, and for a few lines, she was able to join me one last time as I sang it. That was the last time I saw her alive.

So, as I write this, yesterday was her funeral. I'd never been to an Amish funeral, and that's what I started out to write about in this post… But I think I'll save the description of my first Amish funeral for another day, and let this post be about a lady I came to care about greatly, and her large extended family, who became like family to me.

I plan to return to this living room at Steve's house regularly, because Steve and Martha have become dear friends, as have many other members of Mrs. R.'s extended family. So in that way, she will keep on giving to me, far in excess of what small comfort I could give to her. I will never forget her.

My First Amish Funeral

A few days ago I went to my first Amish funeral—the funeral of my beloved Mrs. R.

Today I'll write about Amish visitations and funerals, using hers as an example. I had my friend Rebecca proofread this to be sure I'm giving a good representation of Amish funerals in general.

The visitation took place over two days at the large "shop building" on her son's farm. As I entered, I saw coffee and homemade cookies, a guest book, and a framed memorial for her late husband, as well as one for her infant daughter Mary who died many years ago. Mrs. R. was married for 29 years, and was then a widow for 31 years. Wow…

I then viewed her in her coffin. She looked lovely—better than she did the last time I saw her. Rebecca told me that typically a black dress is worn for burial, but years ago, Mrs. R. had made a white dress which she wished to be buried in. Along with her white prayer cap, she looked ready to meet her Maker.

After that, I saw her large family sitting on a couple rows of benches facing each other. Other benches were set up behind on one side, for anyone who wanted to stay for a while. Mrs. R. had six sons and six surviving daughters, along with 60 grandchildren, so there were a couple dozen relatives there when I walked along the line, shaking hands and hugging members of the family. I've made a number of dear friends in this clan!

The funeral was held the next day at 9:30 in the morning, in the larger shop building of the farm next door. I sat with my friend Rebecca, who kindly walked me through the whole morning's events. Benches were set up in a U shape, about 10 benches deep on each side, with the ministers at the top of the U shape. It was said that there were 400-500 people present. I sat with the women of the home church district. Mrs. R. had quite a few non-Amish relatives, including four of her sons, so there was a liberal sprinkling of Englishers there. A busload of her husband's relatives from Lancaster County were present. The coffin was closed during the service and was placed in front.

The first sermon was by a minister of the home district and lasted about 20 minutes. I caught enough of it to know that the ten commandments were one of the themes. Then a visiting minister from Kansas (Mrs. R. was born in Kansas) gave a sermon of about 20 minutes. After that, the bishop of the home district gave a sermon of about an hour. Nearly all of this was in "Dutch," so I didn't catch much, but I felt like I needed to be there anyway.

At about 11:00 the pace changed. Firstly, there was a prayer, with nearly everyone kneeling. Then the obituary was read aloud (in English). Then the other minister of the home district read aloud a chapter of Scripture (in the Old German language).

After that, while some of the men sang from the Old German Ausbund (hymnbook), each row of mourners took a turn filing past the coffin, with the relatives coming up last by family groups. As son Steve and his wife Martha stood by the coffin, their faces looking so grief-stricken, the tears started to flow for me and many others present...

After that, the funeral ended. Because the family was so large, quite a number of those present lined up in buggies behind the coffin wagon, or in cars (including mine) for the trip to the cemetery for the graveside service. Arriving at the cemetery, I felt it was okay to take a couple photos, from a respectful distance, with the approval of my ever-present friend Rebecca.

At the graveside the coffin was lowered into the ground, into an open wooden casket, by the pallbearers, and then the lid of the casket was put in place. After that, there were some words from the home district bishop, and then, as some of the men stood by and sang, the pallbearers picked up shovels and began to cover the casket with dirt. Others from the family, mostly young men, took turns with the shovels, until the soil was up to ground level. Then the pieces of sod, which had been laid to one side, were placed over the grave.

While we were at the graveside, the others ate lunch back at the home farm. Then when we returned, we had our meal. This took place in the family shop building where the visitation had been the day before.

I hope this helps you visualize an Amish funeral. It was a new experience for me, but a good and necessary one. Farewell and Godspeed, Mrs. R… I hope to see you again on the other side.

Singing To Katie

I got these flowers the other day from an Amish farm wife down the road. They're fading now, but I wanted to take a picture while I could. Her reason for giving them to me? I've been singing to her daughter.

Katie is seventeen years old. A year ago she turned sixteen and began "running around with the young folks." One of her favorite activities was the Sunday night singings, and soon she knew quite a few of the English hymns and gospel songs by heart.

But last March (it is July 2020 as I write this), she was stricken with paralysis. The cause turned out to be a fast-growing malignant tumor on her spine. The doctors said there was nothing to be done and sent her home—at this point she was given three weeks to live. At first she was paralyzed from the neck down, but lately, she can use her arms and hands again and can sit in a wheelchair, when she feels up to it.

She is in good spirits these days, after some dark times at the beginning. Her faith in God is strong. When she expressed a wish to join the church and be baptized, her Amish bishop expedited the usual instruction sessions. So a couple of weeks ago, she came to church in her wheelchair, affirmed her faith, was baptized at a special service, and became a full member of the Amish church.

I heard about Katie from another Amish friend of mine a couple of months ago. My first thought was, "Maybe I could sing for her, like I sing for Mrs. R." I had met her father last year when I bought some books from him, so I knew where she lived... But every time I thought about driving over there, my cowardice held me back. What would they think?

But my little voice wouldn't let me forget about it, and eventually I listened and pulled into her driveway one afternoon.

The whole family was sitting outside under a shade tree having lunch. I plunged ahead and asked if she would like me to stop by and sing to her some time soon. Both she and her mother said that would be very nice. Whew! I felt good that I had finally listened to my better side instead of my fear.

So, now I stop by their farm with my hymnal nearly every week. Sometimes Katie is weak and bedridden, and the tears in her eyes tell me everything... but sometimes she is stronger and can sit up a little and sing along with me. Sometimes some of her younger brothers and sisters gather around their sister's hospital bed, set up in a corner of the living room along with her oxygen tank.

Her mother tells me how much she appreciates my coming, but I tell her it's my privilege to be allowed to be there! I don't know Katie's future, but I'm glad to be a part of it.

Singing With Katie

When I last talked about Katie it was July 2020… Now it's March 2021—nine months later and about a year since her diagnosis. Contrary to the doctor's predictions, Katie is still alive! As last summer wore on, Katie got stronger and stronger in her upper body. She also got a wonderful new power wheelchair, which allowed her a lot more mobility and freedom. She could even power around the farm and up and down the lane. She no longer needed her oxygen tank, and soon she could sit up better and even move herself from her bed to her wheelchair. She has been making the most of the mobility she has.

So last fall, she got the chance to fulfill a dream and volunteer at the Amish schoolhouse down the road, as a teacher's aide. The teacher for grades 1-4 had her hands full with eight first graders, one of them with special needs. Katie took over the first graders—at first every morning, then all day. Soon she was even staying after school to help the teacher grade the papers. Five days a week... Katie was now busier than I am! Later in the school term, a special education classroom was set up for the special needs child and Katie became his full-time teacher.

Her power wheelchair gets here there every morning—about a quarter mile over a hill. She comes home at noon so her mother can take care of her physical needs while the students have their lunch break; then she goes back for the afternoon. I've stopped by several times, and I attended their Christmas program last winter.

Things have improved at home, also. Thanks in part to a grant from the Make-A-Wish Foundation, the far end of the living room that serves as Katie's bedroom has been expanded and remodeled by Katie's father and oldest brother. It now contains bookshelves for Katie's many books, a wardrobe closet with a low mirror, a desk under one of the windows (there are five windows)—and best of all, a handicap-accessible bathroom with a shower! Katie can now take a long, luxurious shower.

Katie is no longer in a hospital bed—she now sleeps in the double bed from her former upstairs bedroom. One of her younger brothers or sisters often sleeps there with her. When I come over I bring Velcro, my goldendoodle pup, and the two of them get along very well! Velcro snuggles down in Katie's bed and goes to sleep. Goldendoodles are known for being very good with sick or disabled people, so it's a perfect fit.

I no longer need to go over there to cheer Katie up from her sickbed—but I still visit regularly, because Katie and her entire family have become very dear to me. Katie and I have matching hymnbooks. We take turns picking out a song, then she sings the melody and I sing the alto part. We sometimes talk for a long time about her life, my life, and life in general.

One day last fall, my husband and I had the whole family over to our house for pizza—Katie, her parents, and her nine siblings ages two to twenty. It was a lovely evening, and ended with their family gathering around our fireplace and singing Gary and I a song about heaven, in four part harmony. I felt like I was in heaven!

Another time this past year, Katie's parents invited us over for supper. It was amazing to see the long kitchen table with the twelve of them and the two of us, and how well organized everything was—before, during, and after the meal. They had a set of everything at each end of the table, to allow for less passing around of things. After the meal and some good talk, they broke out the songbooks and we sang lots of hymns, in four-part harmony.

Make no mistake, Katie is still a sick girl. She went to Indianapolis several months ago (fall 2021) for scans, and the cancer is still in her spine, and it's still growing (although quite a bit more slowly than the doctors expected), and it's still incurable.

Nevertheless, Katie has been given the gift of life for far longer than anyone had imagined, and it's been a pretty good life in recent days… Only God knows what her future will be, but if there's one thing I have been reminded of by my friendship with Katie, it's to savor life, every single day.

Katie and Joni

Something wonderful is going to happen at my house today—at least, I hope so.

It involves two people in particular: My young friend Katie, who is nineteen, and Joni Eareckson Tada, world-famous speaker, artist, author, and advocate for the disabled, who also happens to be a quadriplegic.

A few more facts: Joni helped in the effort to create the Americans With Disabilities Act, and she was present at the White House for its signing in 1990. She is a popular speaker who once spoke to 100,000 people at a Billy Graham crusade in Hungary. Her organization has provided hundreds of wheelchairs for disabled people all over the world. She has been happily married to Ken Tada, a now-retired teacher and coach, for nearly 40 years.

It all started when I gave Katie a biography of Joni last year. She told me later that at first she couldn't bring herself to pick it up and read it—Joni was paralyzed at the same age Katie was, and the story just hit too close to home! But eventually she picked up the book and read it, and then Joni became her new favorite author. I supplied more of Joni's books (she's written nearly fifty books and sold millions), and then last fall, Katie sat down and wrote Joni a letter.

To her surprise and delight, she got a response. Katie had told her story in the letter, and Joni spoke to that and other personal bits from Katie's letter that showed that she had truly spent time on Katie's letter. Joni also enclosed three more of her books.

Katie was over the moon! I bought her a frame for the letter and continued to supply her with Joni's books.

Then a few months ago, my husband remarked how wonderful it would be if Katie could hear Joni speak somewhere. That got me thinking, so I sent an email to the Joni & Friends headquarters in California, asking if Joni was speaking anywhere in northern Indiana this year.

I got a response from Joni's office that Joni wasn't doing much public speaking these days, but how about a Facetime call between Joni and Katie? Now Katie and I were both over the moon!

But soon I ran into some glitches. Firstly, the cell phone reception out at Katie's farm in the hills is pretty bad, and it was found to be unsuitable for a Facetime call. Solution? We would get Katie and her mother to my place in nearby Middlebury.

But how to do that? The family has a wheelchair buggy, but could a horse and buggy be parked in my yard? I live in a subdivision with an HOA. Solution? We'd take the chance. Sometimes it's easier to ask forgiveness than to get permission.

But where to park it? As I walked around our property, the answer made itself known: Out in the yard, I found an old metal hook grown into a tree.

But how to get Katie into my house? My husband made a ramp which we keep in the barn, but he recently broke his T12 vertebra, so hauling it out with a broken back was out of the question. Solution? Katie's mom said that they had a lightweight, foldable, portable ramp, which she could bring along in the buggy.

So now it's 10:15 on a Monday morning in May… Katie and her mother will pull up with their horse and wheelchair buggy later this morning. After we have some pizza and a look around my woodland garden, Joni will call us from California at 2:00 p.m. Eastern time. All I can do is wait, and pray, and hope I can pull this off.

* * * * * * * * * * *

Later the same day

Everyone has gone home now, but what a special and wonderful day this turned out to be!

Katie, her parents, and her two youngest brothers (ages four and six) arrived in the wheelchair buggy, which we parked in my back yard with no problem. With the ramp they brought, we easily got Katie into my house.

When the Facetime call came, I introduced myself and Katie's family, then handed my iPad to Katie and sat in an easy chair nearby to listen and enjoy. Katie's mom listened from the couch or behind the wheelchair while her father sat nearby, taking notes on everything.

Katie's time with Joni was everything I hoped it would be, and more. Joni has an amazing way of relating to people, and she spent nearly forty minutes with my young friend. It was magical. As I listened to Joni's encouragement and advice and loving concern, I had a hard time keeping back the tears. It's not often that an ordinary person like me gets the chance to help make someone's dream come true.

At one point Joni said, "Would you like to see my art studio?" Joni wouldn't have known this, but Katie loves art and sometimes paints. Joni showed Katie many lovely things in her studio, and even demonstrated for Katie how she paints by holding a paintbrush in her teeth, and how she sticks it in her arm splint when she wants to take a break.

At the end of the call, Joni asked us all to gather around Katie's wheelchair, and then she prayed for Katie and all of her family. It was the perfect ending.

Keeping Vigil For Katie

Saturday, January 28, 2023

As I write this, it's 1:15 in the morning.

A few hours ago I returned from nine days with my sister in California. But I didn't go home to my husband and puppy—not yet anyway... Because while I was gone, my dear young friend Katie finally lost her nearly-three-year battle with cancer of the spine at age nineteen.

So here I sit, in a comfy chair in Katie's old bedroom... But instead of singing to her by her bedside, her bed is now empty—and she lies in her coffin beside me, finally at peace.

Her parents slumber in a bedroom nearby, and her nine siblings are upstairs—except for one brother, who fell asleep on a couch in the living room and was left there, undisturbed.

I've written before about Katie. But how do I write about how much she—and her family—have come to mean to me? I've lost one friend, but I hope (and expect) that her family will be lifelong friends. That's part of the good that came from this tragedy.

But right now I am keeping vigil by lantern-light for my young friend as the night passes on, writing and remembering…

When this chapter in my life began, it was June of 2020 and I began to stop by the Miller farm to sing to seventeen-year-old Katie every week or two. Two years went by, as Katie turned eighteen, and then nineteen.

Then late last summer, after a wonderful train trip to Montana with her family, her mind started to get more and more spotty. Before long, as autumn progressed, her vision slowly disappeared, as did her strength and health. She was moved back into a rented hospital bed and her mother's heavy caregiving load became even heavier.

As the cancer spread and got the upper hand, soon I was singing to her once again, as she joined in on the choruses as she could, but less and less as the autumn wore on and the pain and the headaches and the confusion and the vision loss increased.

Towards the end, it was difficult to know how much Katie heard or understood—but who can know for sure?—so I kept on singing.

Then, not knowing how many more times she'd confound the doctors and stick around, I went to Los Angeles to see my sister Nancy… and now Katie is gone, and I missed the two days' visitation. But tonight as I keep vigil by her side, I'm having my own visitation, and I'm trying to write down even a small fraction of what she meant to me.

In a few hours the sun will come up, and the Amish community (along with a few English like me) will gather for Katie's funeral—a service of worship and remembrance and thankfulness for a precious young lady and a life well lived.

In the meantime, I'm going to pick up the hymnbook her mother left here for me, and I'm going to sing to Katie—one last time.

I last saw Katie alive a few days before I left for California. My new friend "Wheelchair Mary" was also visiting Katie that morning. She

told me how nice it was that I sing to Katie... and that made me
wonder if Mary's days sometimes get long or lonely.

So now I know clearly what I want to do... Next week I'm going to
grab my hymnbook, hop in my Jeep, and head down to sing for
Wheelchair Mary.

In Loving Memory

"Katie"
March 4, 2003 – January 25, 2023

O come, angel band, come and around me stand
O bear me away on your snowy wings
To my eternal home.

Saying Goodbye to Katie

Late Sunday Evening, January 29, 2023

Yesterday I attended the funeral of my young friend Katie… How do I put my feelings about that in words?

So after my all-night vigil, I came home this morning, slept for an hour, put on my best black dress, and went back to their family farm. Although the funeral officially started at 9:30, many buggies were already there at 8:00. I was shown to the large outbuilding where the funeral would take place. The extended family had been there an hour already, saying their last goodbyes.

The seating arrangement at these events follows a certain protocol. I was shown to a special area where Wheelchair Mary and a few other special friends of Katie and the family would be seated. The only other Englishers I could see were Katie's hospice doctor, who sat with his family in front of me. The outbuilding (recently remodeled and updated by Katie's father in time for this event) held perhaps 400 people, and nearby was a second building with hundreds more.

The coffin was closed and the funeral started at 9:30 with a series of two or three sermons and a prayer, all in "Dutch." Then at about 11:00, Katie's obituary was read aloud in English. After that, each section of people in the assembly filed row-by-row past Katie's coffin, now open again, starting with the several hundred who were gathered in the building nearby; then the home church group and other groups in the main building; then the extended family of Katie; then lastly, her parents and nine siblings ages four to twenty-one. Never in my lifetime have I seen such an outpouring of grief... As Katie's parents and siblings gathered around her coffin, hanging on to each other and weeping, I doubt there was a dry eye in the building.

After the funeral, 50 or 60 of us headed to the cemetery while the others shared a meal. Slowly the dozens of buggies entered the road behind the hearse buggy for the several-mile drive to the cemetery on a hill behind an Amish farm, where the grave had been dug and a tent set up. As we gathered around, the minister said a few words, and then—according to Amish tradition—the pallbearers lowered the coffin into a wooden casket which was already in the ground, and the top of the casket was put in place.

Then the pallbearers took up shovels and gently began shoveling the soil back into the hole over the casket. As they grew tired, other men stepped forward to take a turn. Many of the teenaged boys who were present did their part too, as the family stood silently and watched. Then Katie's littlest brother, four-year-old Caleb, stepped forward to take a turn. His 21-year-old brother bent over behind him, helping him hold the shovel and drop the soil down. After that, Katie's other brothers took a turn, as well as her normally shy ten-year-old sister. (Well done, Jane!)

After the soil was replaced and a marker put in place, a few songs were sung—the beautiful harmonies being carried out over the farmland—and then our procession of buggies returned to the home farm for a meal.

Now it's Monday afternoon. Two more days have gone by, and I need to finish this post. Today the family is taking another day to rest. Then tomorrow it's back to school, work, and farm chores.

Last night I drove their three oldest to a Sunday night singing; it was 15 miles each way, in bad weather, so I gave them a lift. They invited me to come back early and listen to the music, and I took them up on the offer. As I sat in the back with the moms, I was especially touched by one of the songs the eighty or so young people sang—so I'll end this story with their words: "When the battle's over, we shall wear a crown, in the new Jerusalem."

I have fought the good fight,
I have finished my course,
I have kept the faith.
2 Timothy 4:7

MORE THINGS I'VE LEARNED

The Dawdi Haus: Retirement the Amish Way

It's 2013 as I write this, and my original Amish friends, Gerald and Rebecca, recently purchased a Dawdi Haus. Most times, however, a Dawdi Haus is built, not bought.

What is a Dawdi Haus? It's a retirement home. In the Amish culture the youngest son normally buys the family farm. If the youngest is in another line of business, another son gets the farm—or even a daughter and her husband. In one Amish family I know, the oldest son ended up with the family farm, so there's some flexibility there. But traditionally, it's the youngest son.

It's a great system, if you think about it... By the time the youngest son marries, probably in his early- or mid-twenties, the parents are most likely in their sixties. So the son and his wife take over the farm, and the parents move into the Dawdi Haus (Grandparent House). Normally this is a second, separate home on the same property as the farm. Sometimes it's connected by a breezeway, but each family unit has their privacy, and each woman has her own kitchen. (Even the Amish believe my father's old saying, apparently—"Two women can't live under the same roof.")

Since the Amish don't take Social Security payments, it's the children's job to care for their aging parents, and this system makes it easier. Help and assistance is close at hand, and loneliness—the bane of the widowed retiree—is kept at bay. The newly retired grandparents can do as much or as little farm work as they choose to do, and as health allows. The grandfather can still help out on the farm, and the grandmother can help with the cooking, grandchildren, or whatever she wants. They are included in family and social gatherings and never feel like they've been left behind. They have their privacy, and their own home, but family is nearby in case of trouble, and they can be properly looked after as they get older. It's a tradition that works well.

Anyway… My original Amish friends recently purchased a Dawdi Haus—as opposed to building or moving into one on their farm.

They had been eyeing the English home next door for a number of years, and when it went up for sale, they bought it to use as their future retirement home. This is out of the norm in three ways: Firstly, it is not on the home property—it is next door. Secondly, it is presently an English house. Thirdly, they are not ready to retire; their youngest son is only fifteen. They will rent the house out for a few years until they need it.

They bought the house from empty nesters who had let it go to rack and ruin, both inside and out. They have already started the process of cleaning it out. I saw it recently, and what a mess! On the outside, they are going to build a small horse barn, but for now, they turned the small yard barn into a horse barn for their renters. There is an in-ground pool which they are filling in. The gardens had been neglected for years. The garage floor and part of the driveway had to be torn out, and their cement-contractor son-in-law is pouring a new floor.

The inside looks like it was done in the 1970s… Old shag carpet which will eventually be torn out—the Amish prefer vinyl flooring since it's hard to vacuum without plug-in electricity. Lots of dated built-ins that were topped with mouse poop. A balcony which had been enclosed and now is home to hundreds of flies. A cramped kitchen which will be a lot more Amish-friendly when a wall is knocked out.

But the house has advantages. It is large and roomy with lots of natural light, and it sits on a hill where it has beautiful views of the surrounding countryside. It will be wonderful when it's done. And best of all, it's next door to the old family farm.

So there's lots to do, but they're up to the task. Right now the house still has electricity; the Amish around here are allowed to take up to a year to remove the electricity from an English home they purchase. In the meantime they are allowed to use it, so they can use power tools (or a vacuum) without having to hook up to a gas-powered generator. I look forward to seeing their progress!

2023 update: You'd never know the place! The main floor has lovely vinyl flooring and a new kitchen designed and built by Gerald (shown here), and the living room wall has been bumped out with a large bay window. There are some new windows in the dining area where some cheap wall cabinets used to be, so now there are lots of nice cross-breezes—important in a home that doesn't have air conditioning. The two tiny upstairs bathrooms are now one much nicer bathroom. The fly-infested enclosed balcony is now open to the fresh air and overlooks the family dairy farm down the hill. The old garage area is a big laundry and workroom where the former kitchen cabinets and countertop were removed, redone, and reinstalled to make a canning kitchen. The exterior siding has been redone. There is a lovely horse barn/workshop at the end of the big new driveway. It is a lovely home!

Keeping Telephones at Arm's Length

It used to be in the 1990s that to communicate with my Amish friends, I'd have to write a letter. And if my Amish friends needed to make a phone call, they would walk or ride a bike to the diner down the road. But these days, land-line phones have worked their way into the Amish community—via phone shanties.

A phone shanty is a little building out by the road containing a phone which several families might share. (No, those are not outhouses!) Each family (or young person) has a different voice mail extension, so this is what you hear: "For Alvin Troyer, press 1. For Merle Beachy, press 2. For Noah Miller, press 3. For Jacob Bontrager, press 4."

When I phone my Amish friends, I leave a voice message. They usually check their voice mail a few times a day and call me back. It's still a strange thing to me to hear my cell phone and see their name on the caller ID! But it does make it much easier to plan things than in the old days.

Some businesses have phone shanties closer to the building. When you see print ads for Amish retail businesses in tourism brochures or

The People's Exchange, a phone number is often listed, but normally it will say "VM" next to the number—"voicemail."

Some Amish businesses are permitted to have cell phones for business, especially builders or other contractors who are "out and about" during the day. And Amish young people ages 16 and upwards who are in their "running around years" (rumspringa) and have not yet joined the church might frequently have cell phones.

Why are phone shanties allowed, but phones inside the home are not? The long and short of it is, the Amish want to discourage faceless electronic communication rather than actual human contact. They also frown on having endless hours frittered away socializing over the phone. Their phones are for necessary calls, so they keep them at arm's length... They believe in doing your work when it's time to do your work, and then when work is done, spending lots of time in social activities and fellowship—face to face and in person.

I remarked to my friend that recently I've seen what I call "phone shanty creep"—the shanties seem to be moving farther up the lane and closer to the homes and businesses. She agreed with that, and said that their church district bishop has said that the shanty can be partially up the lane, but not close enough that you can hear it ring from inside the house.

What a slippery slope keeping modern technology at bay can be! A 500-year-old religious and cultural group, trying to maintain their identity as a "separate people" while not creating undue hardship on their members... But as I've said before, it's not my place to defend the Amish or try to explain their theology. I'm glad they are as accepting of my contradictions as I try to be of theirs!

What Kid Doesn't Want to Sleep in the Yard?

One time years ago when Gary and I visited Amish Indiana for the weekend, we stopped to see our Amish friends, as we often liked to do. Gerald was out in the fields, so we hopped in the Jeep with his wife Rebecca in the back seat and drove out there, down the long, sandy lane to the far end of their deep and narrow acreage. Gerald took a break from his corn-planting, gave the five-horse team of Belgians a rest, and we walked back into the woods, where Rebecca wanted to show us something.

On the way, Rebecca told us that their two youngest sons had always liked to camp out in these woods on a summer night with their friends. They had been doing this for a number of years—but this year, the older brother was sixteen, had a buggy and horse at his disposal, and was old enough to be 'running around' socially. He had other interests now, and no longer camped out in the woods with his friends. But his younger brother Jay planned to do so that very weekend, and had been working with his friends to upgrade the site.

A few minutes into the woods, we saw this wonderful picture. Is there any young boy who likes the outdoors—Amish or English—who wouldn't love this? The boys had cleared an area in the woods,

179

made a fence using a circle of trees, and set up a campfire pit with a cooking area over it. In the right foreground you can see their firewood supply, cut and stacked. Rebecca told us that they planned to come out that afternoon to set up a tent and make other final preparations.

But, boys will be boys... We asked Rebecca what the boys would be cooking over the fire the next evening. She smiled and said, "They told me that what they really wanted was for me to heat up a pizza and bring it out, and they would keep it warm over the fire." Fourteen-year-old boys may like to camp out, but that doesn't mean they know how to cook!

The Amish being a very social people, the plan was that the boys' parents would come along as well, and while the boys camped out in the woods, the parents would socialize at the main house. It sounded like a great plan to me. I hope they had good weather!

Making Amish Buggies

Recently Gary and I were able to spend some time at an Amish buggy maker's shop. We saw buggies in all stages of production.

The supporting frame is made of ash wood; Gary had asked if it was maple, and the proprietor said that maple isn't as strong. Gary grabbed the poles in the front to see where it swiveled. (Answer: behind the front axle.)

The box is made of thick plywood (or sometimes fiberglass in newer buggies). Amish buggies come in three sizes: single, with just one seat; double, with two seats; and queen, which has one seat with an extra storage area behind the seat. But the shape and black exterior is the same for all; that must follow the local church custom or "ordnung."

The customer can choose the upholstery (various fabrics or textured vinyl) from a book of samples. There are various upgrades to the basic buggy available, such as a heater (usually battery), LED lights, fold-down back seats, upgraded windshield glass, and brakes (mechanical or hydraulic drum brakes). Prices vary according to size of buggy and upgrades—but as of 2023 the range is $12,000 to $15,000. A double weighs in at about 1,000 pounds.

The finish on the buggies I saw were amazing—similar in look to an automotive finish. I asked how they turned plywood into something so hard and shiny. They told me that it takes three coats of primer, followed by three coats of polyurethane black paint, or sometimes more.

This particular shop, one of several in the Shipshewana area, makes about two buggies per week, and each one takes about 100 hours of labor to produce. He told us that most of his buggies are sold locally, but some are sent to nearby states such as Kentucky, Wisconsin, and Missouri. There is such a demand for their buggies that this shop's waiting list now reaches ahead two years! Those who are in more of a hurry can go to other local shops with higher prices and shorter waiting lists.

Learning More About Amish Buggies

One time in 2019 I drove a young Amish friend to a buggy shop south of Shipshewana where he was going to order a brand new buggy. He'd been waiting a while, since waiting lists are long at most local buggy shops, but his buggy was going to be built next week, so it was time to go in and work out the details. Just like with cars, there are many options to choose from.

My young friend Jay is 24 and has been a church member for a few years already. His present buggy is three years old, but recently his younger brother, a brand-new church member, bought a new buggy with some nice new options, so now Jay wants one like that! He sold his present buggy at the local Yoder Consignment Auction a few weeks ago and it fetched $7,000+. His new buggy will cost around $10,000—and that's including some nice upgrades.

After we arrived and Jay settled down to talk options with the owner, I wandered around and took a few photos (camera on silent mode).

This young man was working on the upholstery for a buggy—a dark green woven fabric. Buggies can also have vinyl upholstery, usually in a dark color. Tools in the shop were mostly run from an air compressor ("Amish electricity") but battery power is also used.

Three other men were working in the shop while I was there. One was sweeping the floor with a push broom, so I took over and finished that job, to make up for being such a nuisance!

I liked the display of the various dashboard and exterior light options available. There is generally a car-type battery in a buggy, to run the electrical components.

An approaching buggy has yellow flashing lights, and the back view of a buggy shows red flashing lights. There is also plenty of reflective tape on the front and back of newer buggies, as well as other safety features. Some buggies have upgrades such as heat, cup holders, all-metal wheels, a smoother suspension, or a fold-down back seat (if it's a double).

Jay finished his order in about an hour and we were on our way. The buggy will be delivered in a week or two, and I hope it's not long before I get to take a ride in it!

Tying a Paddleboat to a Jeep With Twine in a Blizzard

Sometimes a day doesn't turn out like you planned.

A few years back my husband and I were weekending in Amish Indiana, and we decided to stop and visit my original Amish friends, Gerald and Rebecca. I had left a voice mail for them, saying that we would be in town and if they wanted to go anywhere, if they had any errands, we would be happy to take them for a drive. Gerald called back and said that he'd been wanting to look at paddleboats at the Menard's store in Goshen, and while we were there, why not go out for lunch together?

Goshen, seventeen miles from their farm in Lagrange, is too far to drive with a buggy, especially in a snowstorm. But our Jeep has no problems with the weather, so off we went. Paddleboats are apparently a big thing with the Amish; they use them for an afternoon of fishing on the many lakes in the area. Besides that, their grandkids love them!

Later, at the Menards in Goshen, we realized that the paddleboats were on sale (it being the middle of winter). Adding a 10% off coupon we found to that, it seemed like a very good time to buy. But there was a catch—in order to use the coupon, the boat had to be taken home that day, not delivered at a later date. But how to get it home?

My handy husband went out and took a look at the Jeep and then came back in the store and said, "I think we can get this thing home for you." There followed a flurry of activity by Gerald, my husband, and several Menard's employees. In the end, the boat was held on top of the jeep by twine and not much else, and off we went.

Slowly and carefully, we drove the seventeen miles back to the farm, my husband keeping the car as steady as possible—especially on turns!—while the other three of us looked up at the boat out of the windows, watching for slippage. The snow came down, the plastic flapped in the wind, but boat stayed put.

It wasn't our fastest trip across Amish Indiana, but it worked. We unloaded the boat at the farm an hour later and congratulated ourselves on a job well done. Gerald got the boat at a very low sale price and didn't have to pay for delivery.

The last I heard, he was looking forward to using the boat the following summer on the lake near two of his children's homes. He has outfitted it with an anchor, and some straps to attach it to another paddleboat in case of a group fishing expedition. Maybe my husband and I will take it for a spin some time.

Celebrating Christmas—
But Also Old Christmas

So, I noticed this sign the other day... What exactly is "Old Christmas"?

Turns out it's what the Christian church calls "Epiphany"— twelve days after Christmas and the traditional date of the Three Wise Men coming to Bethlehem to find the infant child Jesus. The Amish all over North America celebrate it as a major holiday. Amish businesses are always closed, as well as those mostly staffed by the Amish.

For more details, I turned to a couple of websites.

"Der Dutchman News" says that throughout the Middle Ages, Christmas was a twelve-day feast which began on December 25 and ended on January 6—thus the song, "The Twelve Days of Christmas." But with the adoption of the Gregorian calendar in place of the old Julian calendar in the 1500s, Pope Gregory XIII declared that December 25 was to be celebrated as Christmas Day. Some Protestant groups, including the Amish, rejected that decree and continued to celebrate Christmas on January 6. These days, the Amish celebrate both days, while the rest of us stick to December 25.

The Amish, however, keep their December 25th celebrations much plainer and simpler than ours. Gifts are exchanged, but in a very low-key way compared to our excesses. There are no Christmas trees or decorations in the house, and no Santa Claus. The day is mainly for food and family gatherings, in addition to celebrating the birth of Christ.

North Country Public Radio's website says that both holidays are for visiting and eating, but one thing sets the two days apart: "Old Christmas is a fasting day, which means that you fast until noontime, and so as one person told me, "It's more fun to go visiting on December 25th, because then you're not fasting in the morning—you get started celebrating from the time you arrive!"

Generally speaking, the Amish celebrate our religious holidays—Good Friday, Easter, Thanksgiving, and Christmas—but the patriotic ones, not so much. They may get the day off work, but they don't do anything special.

Downsizing the Amish Way

Whenever I saw a poster in our community for an Amish retirement or estate auction, I thought, "How sad! They must not have had a single son or daughter who was interested in taking over the family farm!" But I was mistaken.

Now that I have seen the process up close, I understand it better. The bottom line is this: If a family has eight children, it wouldn't be fair to just give the house and farm and livestock and equipment to the youngest son! So, the son who takes over the farm actually purchases the farm from the parents… and if he wants the livestock or equipment, he bids on it at the auction, fair and square.

I was told that if the other bidders recognize that son as being a bidder on something, often they will back off and let him have it without running up the price. What a nice custom!

Anyway, we found ourselves at the retirement auction of our Amish friends Gerald and Rebecca. It was a huge affair, many months in the planning. For the larger outside items—which included three sets of work horses, three buggies, and lots of farm equipment—the auctioneer worked from a booth built into the back of a pickup truck. It was very well designed, with a cabin for the auctioneer and the record-keeper, and built-in speakers on every side. The truck could be moved down the rows as the items came up for sale.

There was also an auction going on all day in one of the larger outbuildings, with all kinds of household things and smaller items. Rebecca told me that she took perhaps three-quarters of her household things with her to their new place next door, so the other 25% were here. I have noticed on many occasions how much more money can be made from an auction compared a traditional estate or yard sale. It's a great way to build a nest egg for the newly retired couple and downsize at the same time.

The son who is taking over the farm bought plenty, as you can imagine. He bid on all three teams of horses, and got two of them— the other team, which he had worked with since his youth, went to a higher bidder from Michigan. One of the daughters of the family bought one of the Amish buggies—it's also going to Michigan, where they live. Another daughter bought quite a bit of the old living room furniture.

All the family and friends were there, and there was good food served all day at reasonable prices in the large room at the back of the house where church is held. Next time you're in Amish Indiana with a few hours to spare, look for a sign like this one. These retirement auctions are fun!

Where Can an Amish Kid Find a Good Volleyball Game?

I stopped in at the Cove a few weeks ago. I've often taken Amish kids there for Saturday night volleyball and socializing—but I've always wanted to get in there when it was empty so I could take some pictures, and this was my chance!

The manager of the Cove, an Amishman named Harley Yoder, was there to show us around and answer our questions. I also owe a thank-you to the November 2019 issue of "The Connection," a newsletter which had a feature article on the Cove.

The official name of the facility is "The Cove Plain Community Youth Center." It is one of a number of such places found in Amish Indiana and southern Michigan (what we here call "Michiana"). It was built in 2015 on four-acre plot and was funded by donations. Since then, it has been self-supporting.

Recently, ten more acres were purchased and two beautiful softball diamonds were added to the campus.

What is the purpose of the Cove? According to Mr. Yoder, there are around 3,000 "youngies" (Amish youth ages 16+) in the area. The Amish community wanted to provide a place for youth activities, socializing, and special events.

Entering the front portion, there is a dining area with tables and booths. Off to one side are restrooms, and nearby is a food concession area. To the left of this area, the rest of the front portion is a large room for relaxing and socializing, with a fireplace, couches, tables and chairs, and game tables. This front portion of the building is 60 by 80 feet.

Proceeding through to the larger back area of the building, there is a beautiful gymnasium, normally set up for volleyball but also equipped for basketball and other sports. The gymnasium is 100 by 110 feet with a 29-foot ceiling.

A big whiteboard gives notice of the many activities going on at any given time, including volleyball, softball, basketball, chess, corn hole, and rook. Saturdays are tournament days, and Saturday night is open gym night.

The youth center operates under a seven-man board and is staffed with volunteers—two or three couples per evening—who prepare and sell food. Mr. Yoder says he is very thankful for the 200+ families who volunteer there!

Michael's Long Night in the ICU

One time Gary and I were weekending in Amish Indiana, getting quotes from several metal fabricators on an aluminum box that he wanted to have custom-made for his hot rod trailer. Our Amish friend Gerald took us to three local Amish-run places, and after we made the rounds, we went out for supper with him and his wife Rebecca at an Italian place in the next town. Rebecca mentioned a recent event that nearly ended in tragedy.

It seems that their sixteen-year-old son Michael was out in the gravel driveway a few days earlier. Several of their buggy horses were hitched there, and the young man reached over to pet one of them.

To digress for a moment: Buggy horses are not all the same in temperament. I know this from reading the "horse for sale" ads in "The People's Exchange." Some are very good-natured and laid back. They are described in the ads with phrases like "broke safe for

194

women to drive" and "completely traffic safe and sound." But others are more high strung and unpredictable. They are often described with words like "a little uneasy at corners" and "does shy at things beside the road."

Back to my story: The horse Michael was petting was of the first type. But standing near that horse was another horse—one they had just acquired from one of their married daughters. She had told them to be careful with that one, as it could be skittish. When Michael petted the first horse, it jumped a little, startling the second horse—who lashed out with both back legs. (And this horse was shod with steel horseshoes, being a buggy horse.) Michael was right in the path of those legs, and he took a hard kick to the gut and fell to the ground.

Fortunately, Gerald was nearby and saw his son crumpled on the ground. When Gerald turned him over, the boy Michael had a deathly pallor and looked as if he was dead—but after what probably seemed like an eternity to his dad, he started choking and gasping and caught a breath. But then he immediately started vomiting and couldn't stop.

One of his parents rushed to the phone shanty and called for a hired driver, and soon they were on their way to the local trauma center. Not long after that, the three of them were en route to South Bend in an ambulance. That must have been the longest 53 miles they could remember!

Once in South Bend, Michael was given a CAT scan, which showed internal bleeding, and then put in the Intensive Care Unit. His blood count for a certain enzyme which should have been about 40 was at 1200 and rising. The doctors said if it didn't come down during the night, it might be fatal.

By the next morning Michael was rallying, and later that day he was sent home and told to rest. I saw him briefly not long after that, and he seemed none the worse for wear and had a smile on his face. But I would imagine that every time his parents look at him, they breathe a silent prayer of thanks for their youngest child and the doctors who took care of him.

Doing Some Shopping for Junior

So I was headed to Warsaw, Indiana the other day, to shop for books at the local Goodwill store there, when I got a call from my husband. He's been doing a lot of driving and hauling for a young Amishman I'll call "Junior."

Junior is busy from before sunrise to early evening these days, and being a bachelor, he has no one to shop for him. So my husband asked me, "While you're at Goodwill, Junior wants to know—could you pick him up some shirts?" (Amishmen wear specially-made pants and jackets, but they can buy their shirts off-the-rack.)

I said I'd be glad to, and Junior got on the phone and gave me the proper size. He said he wanted 10 or 20 shirts—long sleeve and short—if I could find them. I told him it was half-price senior day at Goodwill, so I'd do my best!

Once I got there, I realized this was going to be a bit of a challenge. Amishmen wear only solid colors—no prints or stripes or patterns of any kind. Also, they had to be button-down-the-front shirts—no t-shirts, no polo shirts, no pullovers. Luckily he said any color would do, so that helped.

When I looked at the short-sleeved shirts, it was pretty discouraging; not a single one in his size met the requirements. Anything solid-color was either a polo shirt or a t-shirt. So, onward to the racks of long sleeves.

I had much better luck there. Lots of dress shirts from famous brands—and with my half-price discount, they were only $2.50 apiece. I started finding shirts his size in solid colors, and came up with about a dozen. A couple of them were thicker and softer, which I thought would be good for working outside. I tried to get easy-care fabrics… a few of the selections were silk, which I could not see his Amish landlady washing and wringing and hanging on the line!

I got half a dozen more in the next shorter sleeve length, which he said he could use by having the sleeves cut short and hemmed.

When I gave the bags of shirts to him later, I said, "There are plenty of colors here, especially blue." He said, "Why do men wear so many blue shirts, anyway?" I answered him, "Because blue looks good on almost any man. In fact, when you have your first date with the future wife I'm praying for, wear a blue shirt!" That brought a laugh. (I was serious about the prayers, though.)

All in all, it was a lot of fun. I think I should hire myself out as an Amish Personal Shopper for men who need shirts. It was nice to be able to help him out—and I hope he can use the blue ones soon!

VISITING
AMISH INDIANA

Making Amish Indiana Even Better:
The Pumpkinvine Nature Trail

Gary loves to ride his bike, and I sometimes can be talked into going with him, if he slows the pace to accommodate me. When Gary and I started coming here together in 2007, a bike path was one of the few things Amish Indiana lacked. But no longer.

Piece by piece, a trail has been put together to stretch nearly 20 miles from Shipshewana at the east end, west through Middlebury, then southwest to Goshen. From Goshen riders can hook up with Elkhart on another bike trail. At least five public parks along the trail provide parking and restrooms. All in all, a beautiful ride through Amish Indiana.

The Shipshewana-to-Middlebury stretch, over seven miles long, was mostly completed in the fall of 2012, with one stretch still on public roads at the start. At that point the trail started out at the west edge of Shipshewana and ran eastbound, parallel to State Route 20, towards Middlebury. It is a beautiful trail from the start, as you can see.

It is now 2023, and the entire stretch between Shipshewana and Middlebury is off-road at last. The trail has also been extended from its former terminus on the west side of Shipshewana, and now continues a few more blocks further eastward to end in downtown Shipshewana at North Park.

If you head west from Shipshewana to Middlebury and go a few more miles west after the trail comes out of the woods at the Dairy Queen, it passes alongside Middlebury's Krider World's Fair Garden, which is a wonderful shady spot to take a break before heading back to Shipshewana.

The trail has been a boon for the local Amish population, who can ride their bikes in a safer environment than a country road provides. One of our Amish friends who was in his eighties used to ride the trail from Shipshewana to Middlebury on his bike, where he would treat himself at the Middlebury Dairy Queen before heading home to Shipshewana. But lots of Englishers use the trail too, both locals and tourists, for riding and walking.

You can get more information on the trail's website; google "Pumpkinvine Nature Trail" for the latest. Bikes can be rented at a number of places along the trail.

Photography in Amish Country:
Should I or Shouldn't I?

What about photography in Amish Indiana? When doing private or bus tours, Gary and I get asked that question a lot. Is it against their religion?

The short answer is, yes. They consider photography to be vain and physical-appearance-centered. They also have a stricter interpretation about the commandment concerning graven images than the rest of us do. Even their state-issued ID cards often don't contain a photo.

However: the main issue for them is taking a photo that includes an Amish person's face, especially a church member. For that reason, don't ask them to pose for a photograph, or take any photographs that include their faces.

When six of my Amish friends came to our wedding in suburban Chicago in 2007, one of them went to the wedding photographer before the service and asked him not to take their pictures. Yet I have taken pictures on their farms—of scenery, buggies, animals, gardens, and the interior and exterior of the buildings—with no issues. If I am taking a picture of something on an Amish farm, and any of my friends are in the shot, they will either turn their backs to the camera or step out of the picture.

So are lots of non-offensive photo opportunities in Amish Country! Keep these in mind:

- Plowing, planting, baling hay—any type of field work
- Maple syrup buckets on the trees in spring
- Animals in the pastures, especially baby animals
- Amish school houses (not during school hours)
- Interesting items in stores and bakeries (turn sound off)
- Roadside produce stands
- Interesting signs
- Picturesque barns and homes
- Flower and vegetable gardens
- Sunsets
- Buggies on the road
- Laundry on the clotheslines
- Phone shanties by the road
- Horses and buggies in parking lots (especially at E&S Bulk foods)
- Quilt gardens or barn quilts
- Exteriors of interesting buildings
- Yards full of buggies for church on Sunday mornings
- The 16 Walldogs murals in Shipshewana
- Colorful fall foliage
- Winter snow on fields and farms
- Krider World's Fair Garden in Middlebury—beautiful!

One time when I was writing about Amish gardens, I stopped at an Amish farmhouse where the wife was sitting out in the yard at a picnic table, and I asked her if I could take a few photos of her garden. She said "Sure!" and we ended up sitting and talking fifteen or twenty minutes. This has been a common experience for me when taking photos here. I've had no problems taking photos on Amish farms or anywhere else, as long as I'm respectful.

I find that when I'm taking shots with my phone, it's best to stay back, get the shot quickly, and move on! Later, on my computer, I can do the cropping that saves the part of the image I wanted. If I'm at a farm and there are any Amish people nearby, I let them know that

I'm not including them in my photo. If I am in a store and people are nearby, I turn off the sound on my camera.

I have taken a few photos of Amish folks from a distance, such as farmers working in the fields, but I try to be quick and discreet and usually take the photo through my car window. It's just not worth the chance of being seen as another annoying and intrusive Englisher who doesn't respect their beliefs—especially since I live here now.

Remember as you drive through the countryside, when you see something photogenic, shout at your husband as loudly as you can, "Wait!! Stop!! Pull over!!" At least, that's how I usually do it… Or you could carefully slow down and look for a safe spot to pull over, not on the far side of a hill or curve in the road, and not in someone's driveway. Then turn on your four-way flashers; watch out for traffic when exiting your car; be sure there are no Amish people in the shot; and make some photo memories.

The Ten Commandments of Shopping Here

My husband and I used to visit Amish Indiana mostly to feast—and to feast our eyes—but we also did some shopping. Over the years I brought home gardening supplies, plants, bird feeders, yard art, furniture, house décor, clothing, quilted items, books, and who knows what else? So I thought I would share The Ten Commandments of Shopping in Amish Indiana. These are just my opinions, though, so do whatever you like!

Commandment #1:
Check the current Shipshewana Visitor's Guide. It's free and available everywhere, including online, and it contains the popular and pricey places that most tourists like, but also some great out-of-the-way places. Or stop by the Visitor's Center, on State Road 5 south of downtown.

Commandment #2:
Don't load up at the first place you stop. This holds true for bakeries especially. There are so many good places to explore, so pace yourself! Stop at lots of places. Try some new ones. And save the big tourist places for last—they're often open later.

Commandment #3:

The further you get from the tourist traps, the better the prices. Taking the time to do your homework—or just cruising around the countryside with your eyes open—can save you some money. If prices matter to you more than convenience does, do some exploring before you buy.

Commandment #4:

If you see a homemade sign by the road advertising something you might be interested in—pull over! Drive up the lane and check it out. They wouldn't have the sign out there if they didn't want you to stop by.

Commandment #5:

If you like yard sales at home, check them out on the road. I've come home with all kinds of things from yard sales in Amish Indiana.

Commandment #6:

If you like auctions at home, try to find one here. Pick up a free copy of The People's Exchange (available everywhere) or check bulletin boards in the smaller stores and restaurants. If you see auction signs and a whole lot of buggies and cars gathered at a farm, pull over! We don't often buy, but we love to watch. And there's often food available, usually as a fundraiser for a local Amish school.

Commandment #7:

Bring a cooler! There is a lot of good food here—including things like meat, cheese, and pies which require a cooler—and it's a real shame to pass up something good for want of a cooler. A bag of ice is only a couple of bucks, so bring a cooler!

Commandment #8:

Bring home something yummy to share. I used to bring home goodies for my elderly mother. Many places have small loaves of bread, mini pies, smaller packages of cookies, and other things that make great gifts—so for a few dollars, you can make someone at home very happy.

Commandment #9:

Don't assume that anything you find is locally made. If it doesn't say so, then it's not! Local stores, especially in the main shopping district, are full of low-quality imported and mass-produced items, because many tourists don't know the difference (or don't care).

Commandment #10:

Try someplace new every time you go. No matter how often I went to Amish Indiana as a tourist, we never ran out of new places to shop. Every country road has a bakery, or a farm stand, or a sign advertising bread or eggs or honey or maple syrup or candles or something other good thing.

So there you have them... The Ten Commandments of Shopping in Amish Country. Go and sin no more.

Don't Come to Amish Indiana
(Yes, You Read That Right)

It's the end of an old year and the beginning of a new one as I write this, and I want to start out by clearing the air... This is going to be my grumpiest post ever—but it expresses thoughts that have been on my mind lately.

I named my Facebook page and website and book and tour guide service "My Amish Indiana" for one reason: This reflects my point of view, my experiences, my feelings about my favorite place and new home—Amish Indiana. The culture is dramatically different here than it is in most of America, and it's often unfairly represented in the media and quite misunderstood.

So, agree with me, bear with me, or—if you disagree—it's a free country. But please don't be offended. We're all friends here!

* * * * * * * * * * * *

Don't Come to Amish Indiana

Don't come to Amish Indiana if the slow pace of life frustrates you. Businesses close early here. They close on Sunday. There's little or no fast food. There are no movie theaters here, no big box stores, and very few chain stores or restaurants. The pace on the road is slow. The buggies move 10-15 miles per hour, and the rest of us adjust, passing when we safely can.

Don't come to Amish Indiana if you don't want horse manure on the undercarriage of your car, or if gravel roads bother you. This isn't a place for fancy cars, fancy shoes, or white pants! Here's a perfect example: My husband sold his Corvette after we moved here and bought a Jeep Wrangler.

Don't come to Amish Indiana if you think it's wrong or abusive for the Amish to keep their children out of high school and college. Amish kids are the happiest, most well-adjusted, most mature children I've ever seen—and I taught fifth grade for nineteen years back in suburban Chicago. Besides, take note that the Supreme Court sided with the Amish on this one in 1972, ruling that an eighth-grade education is quite sufficient for an Amish child. And any Amish kid who leaves and wants to pursue higher education simply gets a GED (there are local classes for that).

Don't come to Amish Indiana if you think the countryside is full of "puppy mills." No doubt there are bad apples in the barrel, but that doesn't make all Amish kennels puppy mills!... Many of the larger kennels have in-floor heating, air conditioning, in-house labs for health testing, puppy playgrounds, and filtered water. One of our friends raises puppies and last year he got a perfect 100% on his FDA inspection. His kennel is also certified by both Canine Care and ICAW (the Indiana Council on Animal Welfare). We've been in other kennels, large and small, but just as well-kept. To judge any religious or ethnic group as a whole based on the bad behavior of a few is just not right. Go after the bad ones for sure, but don't malign the good ones. Enough on that subject, which is one of my pet peeves!

Don't come to Amish Indiana if you don't understand the inherent dangers in farming life. Farming is statistically one of the most dangerous occupations in America. On farms, injuries and accidental deaths are a regular occurrence. On the road in buggies, injuries and accidental deaths are a regular occurrence. When people work around horses or other large animals, injuries and accidental deaths are a regular occurrence. That's farm life—it's hard, and dirty, and dangerous. It's one of the main reasons my ancestors (and probably yours) left their farms and moved into town.

Don't come to Amish Indiana if you expect other subcultures to live by your standards of health, education, religion, or anything else. The Amish are not like you and me. They follow a unique religious and cultural tradition that is precious to them and for which many of them died in the old days. But they love their families, and they love God, and they do the best they can to make good decisions every day. I'm glad they don't judge me for some of my cultural choices, and I know that I have their trust primarily because they know I'm not judging them.

Don't come to Amish Indiana if you believe everything you've seen on the internet about "shunning" or "rumspringa." Both are a real part of Amish culture, and I could talk all day about either one. Suffice it to say that shunning is rare and used only as a last resort. And rumspringa—even here in northeastern Indiana, which is known for having a some very wild youth—is pretty laid back for most kids.

So, I hope I haven't offended too many of you, but it was time to clear the air. Remember—not every vacation destination is for everyone!

Bonneyville Mill—
Why Didn't I Visit Sooner?

For many years I visited Amish Indiana as a tourist, before retiring here in 2017. Once in a while a local would say, "Have you visited Bonneyville Mill?" and I thought, "Why would I visit a mill?!" But eventually I ended up there one Sunday afternoon, and now I'm a fan.

It's not just a mill! I had no idea… Their brochure says there are 222 acres of "gently rolling hills, woodlands, marshes, and open meadows," and there are five miles of hiking trails running through them. The gardens are beautiful. There are picnic tables throughout, and five reserve-able shelters (each with picnic tables, water, grills, and restroom facilities). Nice!

Bonneyville Mill is the oldest continuously operating grist mill in Indiana. In its long history it has produced stone-ground flour and other products from all kinds of grains. The original owner, Edward Bonney, hoped his mill would be the center of a thriving new city— but the railroads bypassed Bonneyville and a proposed canal was never built. Edward sold the mill, went into the tavern business, got accused of counterfeiting, and fled town as an outlaw. "O how the mighty have fallen!" as King David said.

Recently I was out there again for our annual church picnic, and I took some pictures. A park employee explained how the mill works, and then cranked it up and grinds some grain. There are helpful displays to explain the process.

Walking upstairs, the 'works' can be seen up close. It's amazing how many of the elements are made of wood, and yet they still hold their own after almost 200 years. Edward Bonney's men knew what they were doing!

Walking downstairs and outside, the actual turbines (water wheels), millrace, and dam can be seen. Everything is well explained, and there are self-guided tour guides available for those who are interested in the mechanics of the thing. It was actually quite progressive for its time, with its unusual horizontal water wheel.

The mill is open to the public, free of charge, on Wednesdays through Sundays from May through October, usually 10 a.m. to 5 p.m. Get more updated information by googling "Bonneyville Mill County Park."

Rollin' Like a Tourist

So, Gary and I decided to take care of some errands the other day, and it turned into a very nice day out in Shipshewana. We were tourists here (well, first me, and then us) for thirty years before we moved to Middlebury six years ago, so we've seen it from both sides. I'd forgotten how nice a few hours in Shipshewana can be!

First we went to one of our favorite eating places Shipshe—Millie's Market Cafe on the top floor of the Davis Mercantile. As usual, the service was excellent, as was the food. I got the grilled cheese sandwich from the children's menu, and Gary got the roast beef.

There's an awesome candy store on the third floor of Davis Mercantile too, and my husband would never let that get past him, so soon I was walking out with a pound of dark chocolate covered nuts and a smile on my face.

I'm a new grandma these days—a real treat, since I didn't get married until I was 52 and I thought that ship had sailed! On the last visit to suburban Chicago to visit the grandkids, I brought along a 50-piece jigsaw puzzle. I've never done a jigsaw puzzle in my life, so I figured my 3-year-old grandgirl and I would be on equal footing!... We had lots of fun with it, so from now on, I'm "The Grandma Who Brings a

Puzzle" and I wanted to get one at the toy store across the hall from Millie's. That toy store is absolutely amazing!

Didn't find the puzzle I wanted, though, so the next stop was the actual puzzle store on the second floor of Davis Mercantile. What a dizzying array! Not a lot of puzzles for young children, but I did find two excellent ones, 60 pieces each, for myself and the grandgirl.

Next stop was the excellent Lang Store on the main floor. Every fall we get a wall calendar there—something beautiful to hang in the wooden calendar holder near our kitchen cabinets. As always, we found a great one there.

Back in the Jeep... I had wanted to check out the new consignment clothing store in town, so Gary dropped me off there next, while he went over to Yoder's Meat and Cheese. The consignment store is new (2022) and is run by a couple of Mennonites. They have both Mennonite and Amish specialty clothes, and also regular English clothes. I walked out with a new shirt and a promise to myself to do a blog post on the store one of these days. It's called Graceful Threads Consignment, and it's located on State Road 5.

Next stop was Yoder Popcorn, at their beautiful new store south of downtown at the corner of 5 and 20. Their microwave popcorn with butter has spoiled us for all other popcorn, so we try to keep a few boxes in the cabinet, and our supply was dangerously low! Yoder Popcorn used to be a few miles south of Shipshewana, but that location is now a veterinary clinic, and they have a new location closer to town.

And last but not least, Gary has been wanting an old pot or pail for a mum we bought, and I'll take any excuse to go to my favorite Amish antique store/junkyard, Glicks—"where buggies go to die." Seems like a strange stop for a typical tourist, you say? Perhaps so, but I have had three different private tours where the visitors specifically asked that I take them there—and they all loved it! This time, Gary found his pail, and I couldn't leave without some more "rusty junk" for my garden.

On the way home, Gary helpfully pointed out that the big round thingy in the photo wasn't going to stay vertical in my garden—where I wanted to set it up to add height to the area—and he suggested I might want to have a big spike or something welded to it, to use as a stake in the ground.

We are familiar with at least four good Amish welding places in the area—Six Mile, Architecture, Hilltop, and Shady Lane—so this time, we stopped at Shady Lane, which is right down the road from where we live in Middlebury.

Fifteen minutes later we drove away with a long spike welded to one
edge of the wheel and only $10 poorer—after talking a bit to the
owner about the recent and tragic death of his wife at age 51. They're
a good family and my heart hurts for them.

Soon we were back home in Middlebury, remembering why we used
to spend weekends out here! Our tummies were full and Gary had a
2023 calendar, sweets, some ground sirloin, cheese, and an old
bucket. I had chocolates, puzzles, a new shirt, popcorn, and rusty
junk. It was a very good day!

For More Information

I hesitate to include links here, because links change and break! Instead, google these terms and you'll be sent to the right place.

For information on the Lagrange/Elkhart County Amish settlement:

Google "My Amish Indiana" to find my website, my social media pages, and information on tours.

For information on tourism in the Shipshewana area:

Google "Lagrange County Convention and Visitor's Bureau."

**For general information on the Amish--
These are the sites I consult when I need information:**

Google Erik Wesner's website at "Amish America."
Google "Amish Studies-The Young Center" at Elizabethtown College

Afterword

I wrote some of these stories ten years ago. Others I wrote very recently. All were originally written for my blog, where I have written over 200 posts so far, and were selected and edited and updated for this book.

If there's one thing I've learned about Amish Indiana, it's how much I still have to learn! Some things I've written here could have changed by the time you read this, or will change—either slowly, church district by church district, over many years, or perhaps more rapidly.

For instance, tractors are working their way into the Amish culture here, some years after skid steers did. Cell phones are starting to be allowed for church members who have a good reason to have one, instead of just young people who haven't joined the church. The closed buggies which owned the road a generation ago remain much the same in look, but materials such as fiberglass are replacing wood, and the electronics are getting more sophisticated. Open-top buggies are more and more popular—something that disappeared here a century ago, but lately has made a huge resurgence.

The people in this book have given their permission for me to tell their stories. Where appropriate, I have changed names or other identifying details. But all are true stories of our life here, told the best I know how to tell them. Thanks for coming along.

And thank you, Nancy, for being the best sister ever, and for encouraging me to write this book.

Made in the USA
Monee, IL
22 April 2024

57292592R10125